D1006659

Opera
Guide 29

Jill Gomez as Flora and Robert Tear as Dov in the world première of 'The Knot Garden' in 1970, produced by Peter Hall with sets by Timothy O'Brien and costumes by Tazeena Firth (photo: Zoë Dominic)

Preface

This series, published under the auspices of English National Opera and The Royal Opera, aims to prepare audiences to evaluate and enjoy opera performances. This particular book was conceived in part as a contribution to Sir Michael Tippett's 80th birthday celebrations in 1985. It is both an introduction and a tribute to his operas.

We are most grateful to The Royal Opera House Trust for making it possible.

Nicholas John
Series Editor

29

The Operas of Michael Tippett

Opera Guide Series Editor: Nicholas John

Published in association with
English National Opera and The Royal Opera
Sponsored by The Royal Opera House Trust

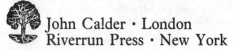

John Calder · London
Riverrun Press · New York

First published in Great Britain, 1985 by John Calder (Publishers) Ltd., 18 Brewer Street, London, W1R 4AS

First published in the U.S.A., 1985 by Riverrun Press Inc., 1170 Broadway, New York, NY 10001

BRITISH LIBRARY CATALOGUING IN PUBLICATION DATA
Tippett, Michael
   The operas of Michael Tippett. — (Opera guides; 29)
   1. Tippett, *Sir* Michael
   I. Title   II. Series
   782.1'092'4   ML410.T467

LIBRARY OF CONGRESS CATALOGING IN PUBLICATION DATA
Tippett, Michael, 1905-
   [Operas. Librettos]
   The operas of Michael Tippett.
   (Opera guide; 29)
   Librettos by the composer.
   "Published in association with English National Opera and The Royal Opera."
   Discography: p.
   Bibliography: p.
   Contents: The midsummer marriage — King Priam — The knot garden — [etc.]
   1. Operas — Librettos.   2. Tippett, Michael, 1905- .   Operas. I. Title.
II. Series.
ML49.T5C3 1985   782.1'092'4   84-1827
ISBN 0-7145-4061-7 (Riverrun Press: pbk.)

SUBSIDISED BY THE
Arts Council
OF GREAT BRITAIN

John Calder (Publishers) Ltd, English National Opera and The Royal Opera House, Covent Garden Ltd receive financial assistance from the Arts Council of Great Britain. English National Opera also receives financial assistance from the Greater London Council.

Typeset in Plantin by Margaret Spooner Typesetting, Dorchester, Dorset

Printed by the Camelot Press Ltd., Southampton

Contents

List of Illustrations

Picture research: Henrietta Bredin

Introduction

Meirion Bowen

No-one examining Michael Tippett's family background and childhood circumstances would be inclined to predict the future emergence of a composer of stature. The Handelian Christian names of his paternal grandfather certainly invite speculation: moreover, George Frederick Tippett (c. 1829-1899) took advantage of his strong tenor voice to dominate the hymn-singing at evangelical religious meetings and even to deputize occasionally for his friend, the renowned 19th-century tenor, Sims Reeves; he also went often to concerts. But none of his musical talents and interests was passed on to his multitudinous progeny (of whom eleven were legitimate, the rest gratuitous products of freelance exertion). His second son, Henry William Tippett (1858-1944) — father of the composer — had neither a talent for music nor much delight in it, though he sometimes went to the opera at Covent Garden and in Paris, and liked to hum *Samson and Delilah*. His talent lay in law and financial investment, as a result of which he was able to retire early. Tippett's mother, Isabel Clementine Binny Kemp (1880-1969) was equally ungifted in music, though she had a penchant for singing drawing-room ballads. Trained as a nurse, she diversified to write novels and plays, join the Labour party and organise demonstrations for women's rights, and generally supported worthy causes: late in life, in fact, she turned to painting, was a disciple of Rudolph Steiner and a vegetarian. Michael Tippett was the second son born (on January 2, 1905) not long after their marriage, his brother Peter preceding him by less than a year. Both were born in London. The family then left their house in Eastcote, Middlesex, to live in the village of Wetherden, Suffolk.

Tippett thus grew up away from the London concert scene and, of course, he was without the alternatives of radio broadcasts and recorded music on tape and disc which were to make life easier for later generations of budding composers. He and his brother were both given piano lessons by local teachers. Tippett himself delighted in improvising at the piano as well as performing party-pieces with manifest aplomb. But neither he nor his parents knew what being a composer meant. A career in mathematics was one he seriously considered. When, for financial reasons, Tippett's parents went to live in France, he was sent to a tough public school near Edinburgh, Fettes College, where sex, sadism and a spartan existence soon caused him to request his parents to come and remove him. He then went to Stamford Grammar School in Lincolnshire, which he enjoyed rather more.

At Stamford, he made considerable progress academically, and became a notorious polemicist, following the example of his suffragette mother and rationalist father by dissenting from the Cadet Corps and established religion. He also advanced his musical experience considerably. He had piano lessons with a local teacher, Mrs Tinkler, who introduced him to Bach's 48 Preludes and Fugues, some Beethoven sonatas and Chopin. He practised enthusiastically. An English teacher, Henry Waldo Acomb, organised concerts at the school and Tippett thus encountered a mixed musical repertoire, ranging from a Mozart piano concerto to folksongs. Acomb involved him in stage productions at the school (he played Portia and Mrs Malaprop) and

7

Tippett even produced some plays himself. Above all, Acomb took him to an orchestral concert in Leicester, conducted by Malcolm Sargent (also an old Stamfordian) which included Ravel's *Mother Goose Suite*: and this first encounter with music by a contemporary caused him to decide immediately that he himself would become a composer.

For a while confusion reigned, as Tippett's parents wondered how to cope with this maverick child, who meanwhile had been expelled from the school for persisting in attempts to convert school friends to atheism. Eventually, as a result of a chance meeting on a train with a Doctor of Music, his parents took him for an interview at The Royal College of Music — the principal, Sir Hugh Allen, despite the boy's musical ignorance, admitted him to the RCM in 1923. Coming to London, where musical and theatrical life was burgeoning greatly after the First World War, offered Tippett many opportunities to explore and study for himself, as well as tuition at the College. The richness of content manifest in the creative works of his maturity owes a lot to his involvement in and fascination with the entire cultural scene at this time. He went regularly to concerts — attending especially the whole Promenade Concert season of 1924 — and to the Beecham seasons at Covent Garden; he was able to hear visiting celebrities perform and conduct — for example, Stravinsky, Ravel, Furtwängler, Chaliapin, the Busch and Lener Quartets. He was also taken to the theatre a lot by friends such as Aubrey Russ and Roy Langford, and thus saw many Shaw premières, plays by Shakespeare, Ibsen and more recent figures. Many specific experiences from this time remained stored in his memory in later years and influenced the conception of his operatic works — seeing Toller's *Masse und Mensch*, for instance, made an impact upon him which, in his seventies, influenced his fourth opera, *The Ice Break*.

At the RCM, he was not regarded as a model student. Although he had a brief but rewarding period of study with Charles Wood, after the latter's death he found himself faced with a choice of Vaughan Williams and C.H. Kitson as possible teachers. Wishing to avoid becoming a compositional acolyte of Vaughan Williams, he went to Kitson whose pedantic approach produced mutual incomprehension and exasperation. But Tippett benefited from conducting studies with Sargent and Dr Adrian Boult (as he then was), the latter encouraging him especially to sit near him at orchestral rehearsals each Friday and observe the performance of music in some detail. The enterprising regime of the RCM in that period also enabled him to become acquainted with several standard operas, as well as new or relatively new works such as Wagner's *Parsifal*, Debussy's *Pelléas et Mélisande* and Vaughan Williams's *Hugh the Drover*. He did a little conducting, but made slender progress as a composer (especially by comparison with such contemporaries as Constant Lambert and Elisabeth Maconchy). In 1928 he failed his B.Mus. examinations; he passed them later the same year, though; and, while his parents had agreed to support him at the RCM on condition he became a Doctor of Music, he now realised he must leave and work at his composition away from the London scene. He was already, by temperament, an auto-didact: he had studied sixteenth-century church music by attending evensong at Westminster Cathedral, having discovered in advance which works were to be performed and copied them out in the RCM library; he had taught himself German (having already been fluent in French since childhood); he had read voraciously — tackling Gibbon's *Decline and Fall*, Frazer's *Golden Bough*, and other literary monuments. In 1924, wishing to pursue his interest in madrigals, he had responded to an invitation to conduct an amateur operatic and choral society in Oxted. After his student days it made sense to live there in a tiny cottage. He could get to London whenever necessary. But now he had the isolation in which to compose. Ever since, he has needed such privacy and silence in which to create, much as he revels in the vitality and tumult of city cultures. He remained, in fact, in Oxted until 1951, then moved into a dilapidated manor house in Wadhurst, Sussex; in 1960 he went to live in an Elizabethen house in Corsham, Wiltshire, but when its surroundings became too noisy (a multi-storey car park was built nearby), he removed to a remote modern-style house in the middle of farmland near Chippenham, where he still resides.

Tippett's individuality and enterprise showed themselves immediately in his work at Oxted. Starting with madrigals, he eventually developed the repertory of his amateur choir, and ultimately they combined with the Limpsfield Players to do stage productions at the recently-built Barn Theatre. They first undertook Vaughan Williams's *The Shepherds of the Delectable Mountains*, in a double-bill with *Everyman*. This was in 1927. The following year, Tippett directed his own realization of the 18th-century ballad opera, *The Village Opera*, and a year after that, Stanford's *The Travelling Companion*, as well as Flecker's *Don Juan*, for which he provided incidental music. Late in 1929, he also conducted another operatic society at the Hackney Institute in London, undertaking Holst's *The Perfect Fool* and, later, Flotow's *Martha*, *Ruddigore* and Sullivan's *The Emerald Isle* (which Edward German had completed). His concerts in Oxted at this time also included a complete *Messiah* (which was later to influence greatly his oratorio *A Child of Our Time*) and, on April 5, 1930, a concert of his own music, involving both his local choir and professional musicians, conducted by a former RCM student-colleague, David Moule-Evans. This latter concert drew appreciative reviews from both *The Times* and *Daily Telegraph*, though the experience was sufficient to convince Tippett that he must study further to advance his control of technique and discover his own musical style. Thus he went to the noted contrapuntal scholar R.O. Morris to study for two years, before continuing original composition on any scale. Although he had a tiny income from his conducting work with amateurs, he had to take a job teaching French in the nearby Hazelwood Preparatory School for boys, in order to make ends meet: and even then his existence continued to be a frugal one for a long time afterwards.

At the school the English master was Christopher Fry, and it was he who subsequently provided the texts for a number of Tippett's vocal works, including some of his earliest efforts at dramatic composition. Tippett also met W.H. Auden, who later introduced him to T.S. Eliot, soon his spiritual mentor. Tippett's coming to maturity as a composer in the 1930s, however, was not so much a consequence of meeting artistic colleagues who were congenial and friends who were intellectually stimulating; it came more from a combination of strengthened musical technique (Morris's disciplines having proved fruitful) and a deepening awareness of human relationships and of current social and political developments. He was especially drawn to three individuals, two contrasted women: Evelyn Maude and Francesca Allinson, and Wilfred Franks, a Bauhaus-trained painter with revolutionary aspirations. The strains and stresses of these relationships underlie the emotional intensity and vibrant spirit of Tippett's String Quartet No. 1 (1934/35; revised 1943), Piano Sonata No. 1 (1936/37; revised 1942 and 1954) and Concerto for Double String Orchestra (1938/39), the first compositions in which the discernibly Tippett-ian voice can be heard.

Hiking with Wilfred Franks into the North of England, Tippett observed for the first time the effects of the Depression and unemployment. He saw children starving. Returning to the well-fed South, he knew that while composition would make him a sort of recluse, he was 'quite certain that . . . somewhere music could have a direct relation to the compassion that was so deep in my own heart.' He left his teaching position at Hazelwood School and took charge of music in the work-camps at Boosbeck, a small mining village in Cleveland, Yorkshire. These camps were created to assist unemployed ironstone miners to survive by nurturing their own land economy and local culture. In this context, Tippett mounted a production of *The Beggar's Opera*. Local people took the leading roles: a milkman played Macheath, a miner's daughter, Polly. The village hall was packed so tightly that Tippett and his small orchestra were pressed up against the stage. The village policeman tried to prevent more people from entering, but an old lady brandished her umbrella at him threateningly and declared (in a strong Yorkshire accent), 'I'll beat your bloody brains in, if you don't let me in!' Tippett had to wait decades for a comparable success in the operatic sphere.

The following year, Tippett collaborated with David Ayerst (who wrote the dialogue) and Ruth Pennyman (who wrote the lyrics) on another folk-song opera, *Robin Hood*, adapting the period subject to their contemporary situation. This, too, was quite a success. It involved the village children in learning Latin so that they could sing the medieval hymn, *Angelus ad Virginem*, at the wedding of Marret (the heroine), and they returned to school for the purpose each afternoon. Although the work is not counted amongst Tippett's mature compositions, some of its material was so distinctive that he felt able to embody it in the Suite in D (written 14 years later for the birthday of Prince Charles): the overture to *Robin Hood,* a 'folk-tune' Tippett had created himself, and other musical ideas from the piece survive in this way.

Returning to London, Tippett continued to combine musical activities with social and political involvements. He conducted the South London Orchestra for Unemployed Musicians, made up of theatre and cinema musicians thrown out of work with the arrival of 'talkies'. He also took charge of two choirs sponsored by the Royal Arsenal Co-operative Society, at first performing political songs but later undertaking light opera, such as *Merrie England*. He joined the Communist Party briefly in 1935, but left after he failed to convert his party branch to Trotskyism. He wrote an anti-capitalist, anti-war play, *War Ramp*, which was performed at Labour Party rallies.

But some of his works written for amateurs in this period were not purely political. For instance, he collaborated with Christopher Fry on two children's operas: one of them, *Robert of Sicily* (1938), was adapted from a poem by Longfellow; the other, *Seven at a Stroke* (1939), had a text by Fry based on a Grimm fairy-tale. These again provided him with lessons in theatrical technique, even though they were not destined to survive as mature compositions. Gradually, Tippett was detaching himself in order to define his own territory as a composer more closely. Thus, although he never lost his sense of social and political commitment, he avoided making music serve ideological ends alone. In essence, his creative position has not changed since the late 1930s. Then he was able to see himself clearly as someone who could create works that would have a value in themselves as art — string quartets, sonatas, symphonies etc. — and, additionally, other works which would have a distinct message or connotations as a public statement. Tippett's career thereafter has entailed keeping a balance between these different

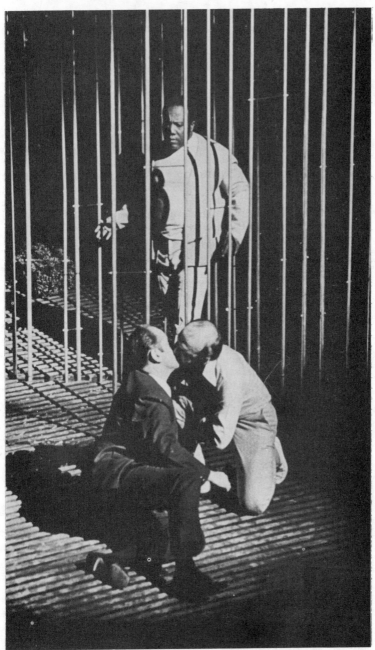

The 1970 world première of 'The Knot Garden' at Covent Garden, produced by Peter Hall, production design by Timothy O'Brien and costumes by Tazeena Firth, lighting by John Bury: Thomas Carey as Mel and (foreground) Raimund Herincx as Faber and Robert Tear as Dov (photo: Stuart Robinson)

11

compositional tasks. In this, he consciously emulated his idol, Beethoven.

The first major work of his to achieve prominence as a public statement was his oratorio, *A Child of Our Time*. This started life as an opera on the Easter Rebellion in Ireland. But it became an oratorio for which, on Eliot's advice, Tippett himself wrote the text. Its immediate inspiration was the shooting of a German diplomat in 1938 by a young Polish Jew, Grynzban, which led to one of the worst of the Nazi pogroms against the Jews in Central Europe. But Tippett wanted to make his oratorio more than a protest, an expression of outrage. He wanted also to demonstrate the power of compassion, tolerance, love and forgiveness. A series of accidents led him to make use of Negro Spirituals at those points in the work where a baroque composer like Bach might have used Lutheran chorales. It was a discerning choice of vernacular material that helped the work, when it was eventually performed, to become one of his most widely loved and appreciated compositions. Since the 1940s, it has been heard all over the world — in Africa, Australia, many parts of the USA, and most recently Tokyo. Interestingly, when it was performed under the composer's baton in Atlanta, Georgia (in 1981), the mainly black audience at each performance joined in the spirituals, just as Bach's congregation would have sung the chorales.

Tippett's humanitarian stance was already made clear when in 1934 he was one of the 100,000 who responded to the Rev. Dick Sheppard's letter to the press inviting those opposed to war to send him a postcard with the pledge: 'I renounce war and never again, directly or indirectly, will I support or sanction another.' Thus was the Peace Pledge Union founded, of which Tippett later became President. In 1943, still stubbornly maintaining his opposition to any wartime activity, he was sentenced to three months' imprisonment in Wormwood Scrubs Prison for failing to comply with the conditions of registration as a conscientious objector. His mother, who had herself endured prison as a suffragette, said this was her proudest moment.

Meanwhile, his musical reputation was growing very slowly. Having become Director of Music at Morley College, he was able to attract many distinguished refugee musicians, such as Walter Goehr, Matyas Seiber, Walter Bergmann, and three members of the Amadeus Quartet (who later joined forces, at Morley, with an English cellist): and the Morley College concerts became some of the liveliest and most imaginative on the London musical scene, featuring rarely heard works such as Monteverdi's *Vespers* (1610), and the Purcell *Odes* (for which Tippett brought along the counter-tenor Alfred Deller, whom he had 'discovered' in Canterbury) and contemporary compositions such as Stravinsky's *Les Noces* and Frank Martin's *Le Vin Herbé*. After having his scores rejected by the BBC, by Boosey & Hawkes and the ISCM, Tippett was eventually taken on by the London branch of the Mainz publishers Schott Ltd. Some recordings appeared and were reviewed, perceptively and favourably, by William Glock, Wilfred Mellers and Edward Sackville-West in particular. But it was still a long haul. The chamber music, songs and orchestral music he was writing in this period depended a lot on the support of sympathetic friends and colleagues. Occasionally, as when (for instance) Peter Pears and Benjamin Britten tackled *Boyhood's End* and *The Heart's Assurance*, the results were elevated, as well as idiomatic.

Throughout the 1940s, Tippett was working towards his first opera. The process was arduous, for it meant reading and researching far afield, then sifting and selecting until exactly the right materials were to hand. *The*

The 1968 production of 'The Midsummer Marriage' at Covent Garden, produced by Ande Anderson and designed by Tony Walton (photo: Houston Rogers, Theatre Museum)

The 1962 première of 'King Priam' at Covent Garden: Hector (Victor Godfrey) leads the Trojans into battle (photo: Donald Southern)

Midsummer Marriage took six years, as far as the writing of the libretto and the composition of the music were concerned: but preceding it were six or more years of preparation. At first it was going to be called *Octett*: his first sketch for it is a diagram linking the seasons to the elements, to musical instruments etc. (see Ex. 1). The project got underway then as a collaboration with a poet-friend (also a conscientious objector), Douglas Newton: whereupon the opera was called *Aurora Consurgens or The Laughing Children*, and a foreword declares its origin in Aristophanes 'as postulated in F.M. Cornford's *Origin of Attic Comedy*'. The Latin part of the title was adopted from *Aurora Consurgens: a Document Attributed to Thomas Aquinas on the Problems of Opposites in Alchemy*, ed. Marie-Louise von Franz. The subtitle was suggested by another conscientious objector, Edric Maynard (who came to work at Doolittle farm, during the early 1940s, near Tippett's cottage in Oxted; he worked in a bookshop and was nicknamed 'The Book Boy'): and it refers to lines in Eliot's *Burnt Norton*:

'Go,' said the bird, for the leaves were full of children,
Hidden excitedly, containing laughter.

The collaboration with Newton did not get very far. Tippett's publisher, Willy Strecker, gave the title of the opera short shrift. Tippett then continued working on his own. He knew it would be his next major statement as a composer. He was currently earning a small secondary income from giving broadcast talks, so gradually he detached himself from Morley College, resigning completely in 1951. *The Midsummer Marriage* dominated his existence. He had no notion of any possible production of the work in the future. Nonetheless, he had to continue. Once he felt so ill working at it, he was sure he had cancer. But this was simply exhaustion, along with a psychosomatic stomach reaction that troubled him for many years afterwards. The opera was at first in two acts, and the Ritual Dances (that were later to assume a life of their own in the concert hall) a mere interlude. The names of characters were also changed as the piece came slowly to fruition: George and Margaret, for instance, became Mark and Jenifer. The final outcome was an opera whose richness of reference, allusion and symbolism was enhanced by music of torrential, lyrical power and clarity.

Not that such qualities were evident from the first production at Covent Garden in January 1955. While many found the music entrancing, only a limited number sensed its dramatic relevance and significance. Much attention was given by the press in advance to apparent bewilderment on the part of the singers. Its obscurity was satirized: 'Not since Salvador Dali tried to introduce a flying hippopotamus into the cast of Strauss's *Salome*' (said *The News Chronicle*), 'has The Royal Opera House had such a baffled cast on its hands as the one which will launch Michael Tippett's *The Midsummer Marriage* into the world tomorrow night.' Reviews were no less condemnatory. Ernest Newman, in *The Sunday Times*, actually admitted that he had written his review before he had heard a note of the music, and pronounced himself unable to make head or tail of it. The *Times* critic wrote (anonymously) that 'Tippett has overloaded his allegory . . . The force behind the conception of the opera had been too much for his control.' Martin Cooper in *The Daily Telegraph* called the libretto 'an extraordinary jumble of verbal images and stage mumbo jumbo.' Cecil Smith in *The Daily Express* declared the libretto to be 'one of the worst in the 350-year-old history of opera.' But there was support from the regular critic of *The News Chronicle*, Scott

14

Goddard, and from a select number of colleagues and friends of all generations. Edward J. Dent, for instance, thought highly of the work, disliking — in his characteristically anti-clerical way — only the Lutheran-sounding chorale that appeared late in Act Three. Amongst younger writers, Peter Heyworth was to write later that the opera 'carries an aura so potent that two or three bars suffice to sweep the addict back into an engulfing world. For me, it has become part of living.'

Tippett was largely unaffected by the harsh criticism of this opera. He preferred to learn the lessons it gave him, both creatively and in his dealings with an opera company. On the one hand, the work was long and much of the dance music had to be cut. The formal proportions of his later operas are (with the exception of Act Three of *King Priam* and some parts of *The Ice Break*) better structured. Tippett also specified too much detail of the presentation in his libretto. Now he is inclined to give more general indications to producer and designer and rely more on their expertise. The original team for *The Midsummer Marriage*, on the other hand, was not ideal. Tippett had wanted it produced by Peter Brook, since he took the view (following Eliot's advice) that opera must relate to the contemporary theatre. Covent Garden's General Administrator, David Webster, had not, however, heard of Brook and there was much procrastination before a house-producer, very late on, was assigned to the work. Christopher West did not thus have time to do it justice: much of Act Three was literally un-produced. Likewise, the designer Barbara Hepworth supplied impressive neo-classic scenery which was impractical to light.

Similar problems affected the second production of the work at Covent Garden in 1968, though by this time, the opera had won wider acceptance, musically, thanks to a BBC studio performance in 1963 conducted by Norman Del Mar, which caught the imagination of innumerable listeners, amongst them the future Musical Director at Covent Garden, Colin Davis. The recording that followed upon the revival of this production became, in the 1970s, a best-seller not only in the UK but particularly in the USA. Since then, there have been outstandingly successful productions of the opera in Australia (1978), at Welsh National Opera (1979), and in San Francisco (1983) where it was regarded as the sensation of the season. Recently the Post Office issued a stamp, commemorating Tippett's achievement in the work.

In the 1960s and 1970s, in fact, Tippett's reputation as a composer grew steadily. The allegations of excessive textural complexity, of over-cerebral deployment of counterpoint, of amateurish orchestration levelled, amazingly, at such luminous works as the *Fantasia Concertanti on a Theme of Corelli* (1953) and the Piano Concerto (1956) all but disappeared. A younger generation of conductors and executants tend now to behave as if such problems do not exist, or, if they do, they can be overcome with the requisite degree of professional rehearsal and commitment. The advocacy of conductors like Colin Davis, Andrew Davis, David Atherton, Elgar Howarth, and of performers like Paul Crossley, the Lindsay Quartet, and Robert Tear, has laid the foundation for a world-wide appreciation of Tippett's quality and stature as a composer. At the same time, from his sixtieth year onwards, Tippett himself has travelled more widely. He quickly established a considerable following in the USA. Not only have a number of American orchestras and universities (sometimes jointly) sponsored Tippett festivals (e.g. Cleveland, Chicago, Los Angeles, San Francisco, Boston) but two of his most substantial recent compositions have been US commissions: Symphony No. 4, commissioned by the Chicago Symphony Orchestra (who gave the première under Solti in 1977) and *The Mask of Time*, commissioned by the Boston Symphony Orchestra (who undertook the première in 1984). In 1978 and 1984, Tippett took extended breaks from composition — his first in well over fifty years of sustained creative enterprise — to travel to the Far East and Australia, conducting and lecturing. The response to his visits (particularly in places like Tokyo) reflected the tremendous, widespread appeal which his music now exerts. Recordings of his music — which became more numerous in the 1970s — of course paved the way.

The three further operas which Tippett has composed since *The Midsummer Marriage* have both fuelled the appreciation of his achievement whilst arousing controversy by moving into new dramatic genres and radically altering the nature of the musical presentation as a consequence. *King Priam*, first produced by The Royal Opera House at the Coventry Festival (arranged to celebrate the opening of the new cathedral there) in 1962, had the kind of producer and designer Tippett desperately wanted — Sam Wanamaker and Sean Kenny, both of them experienced in the world of film and theatre. On David Webster's recommendation, in fact, they had trained the Covent Garden lighting staff in more advanced techniques and the result benefitted their presentation of the new Tippett opera considerably. There were many critics now, however, who — having just warmed to the magic of *The Midsummer Marriage* — were shocked by the hard-hitting, abrasive style of *King Priam*: many of them also have never since welcomed the application of its mosaic-scheme musical structures to Tippett's subsequent, non-operatic compositions. On the other hand, it soon became evident that the work had somehow enabled Tippett's entire compositional manner to crystallise quite decisively. Like all his major 'public' works, *King Priam* had a long gestation — starting as a curious, masque-like composition, entitled *The Windrose*, then turning into a choral work (at the instigation of the Koussevitzky Foundation, who commissioned it), before becoming an opera based on Homer (Tippett having taken advice from Peter Brook and Gunther Rennert). But it was written with much greater fluency than its predecessor. And it enabled him to produce, with enormous self-confidence and assurance, a great outpouring of music of all kinds in the next twenty years or so. Although *King Priam* was revived by Covent Garden a few times, it was only in 1984 that a new and unanimously praised production (by Kent Opera) appeared, although, meanwhile, there was an award-winning recording emanating from the concert performance, in 1980, by the London Sinfonietta and David Atherton.

By the time *The Knot Garden* (1970) and *The Ice Break* (1977) received their premières, also at Covent Garden, there was not much question that Tippett was a force to be reckoned with in the operatic domain. Each new piece seemed to establish new territory. In these two latter works, the speed of the stage-action — reflecting the composer's fascination with television and cinema — engaged the audience's attention, no matter how complex the plots, and went hand in hand with free-ranging music, embodying a wide gamut of stylistic references and quotations. Again, *The Knot Garden* had the benefit of superb partnership in its production team, this time Peter Hall and Timothy O'Brien. *The Ice Break* ran into difficulties, however. Peter Hall had to withdraw quite late on, because of his other commitments. Tippett was in America when this news came through. Soon afterwards, he saw a musical in New York, *Pacific Overtures*, which had the right pace and flair for his opera.

The director of *Pacific Overtures* was Harold Prince, and Covent Garden contacted him with a view to his directing *The Ice Break*. Tippett and the Covent Garden administrator John Tooley even went to see him in Vienna, but by this time Prince had decided against undertaking the work. In the event, it was once more Sam Wanamaker who came to the rescue. Unfortunately there were now serious limitations to what could be achieved in a short time. The production accumulated dancers, directed by the American, Walter Raines; it very nearly entailed holography, but, because of workshop errors, the technological ingredient was limited to laser beams. Nonetheless, the opera was accounted a considerable success at the time, partly because its music was so well realised under Colin Davis (as had been the case earlier with *The Knot Garden*). In retrospect, Tippett feels that he miscalculated some of the proportions of the piece (especially the Psychedelic Trip scene in Act Three) and the speed with which a chorus could be moved around. The opera was subsequently peformed, however, in Kiel, Germany (1978) and under Sarah Caldwell's idiosyncratic direction at the Boston Opera (1979), where it was the best-seller of the season. Even without revisions, it could probably be mounted with some success, if the documentary element in it were regarded as subsidiary to the surrealism called for in the composer's preface. One young producer, invited to direct one of the later Tippett operas, said recently that much as he admired it, he would prefer to do it in 1995, when it would have dated sufficiently!

Tippett's operas are in the forefront of his achievement. But even more than in the case of Britten, his symphonies, sonatas, quartets, song-cycles and major choral works also count for a lot. It is no surprise that from the fifties onwards, he was to receive many public honours and awards, including a CBE in 1959 and a knighthood in 1966; later, in 1979 he became a Companion of Honour, and in 1983 was awarded the Order of Merit: additionally, he has received Honorary Doctorates from 18 British universities, and some abroad, was elected (in 1976) an Honorary Member of the American Academy of Arts and an Extraordinary Member of the Akaedamie der Kunste in Berlin. The same year he received the Gold Medal of the Royal Philharmonic Society — the honour he values above all others, since it came from his colleagues in the profession.

In his eighth decade, Tippett remains in good health, apart from an eyesight problem that has troubled him for nearly fifteen years but which does not seriously interfere with composition. He is currently about to embark on another work for the theatre and his plans for further compositions extend up to 1991. Given his present alertness and sensitivity to all that goes on in the world, he is likely to remain a disturbing, provocative but rewarding composer, hardly likely to fade away into a haze of backward-looking, nostalgic rumination. Most people will continue to find it hard not merely to keep pace with his brand of mischievous and irreverent humour, but to take full purchase on the ideas and prophetic insights which have sustained him as an artist for so many years. A Promenader who attended the European première of his largest work for the concert-hall, *The Mask of Time*, was asked about his reaction in a television news interview afterwards. 'Amazing', he said, 'that man is an incredible dreamer of dreams.'

John Lanigan as Jack and Adèle Leigh as Bella in the 1955 Covent Garden production (photo: Houston Rogers, Theatre Museum)

A Ritual of Renewal

Paul Driver

If I had to recommend an opera to someone innocent of the genre or sceptical about it, I might very well choose Tippett's *The Midsummer Marriage*. Here the rationale of opera is explicit: the characters utter themselves continuously in song, they ride upon a flood of the loveliest orchestral noises, they are enveloped in music and express a dramatic action which could be communicated in no other way. Pure music and pure song, an ecstatic excess of them, become the satisfactions of a developing drama, rehearsed myth and a spiritual message.

Story is clothed from head to foot in song. There is no place for irritable query as to why the characters are singing not speaking; there are no *longueurs* of recitative; and there can be no fretting after fact and reason when the musical thrust is almost physically overwhelming. All the traditional operatic delights are offered: rapturous, even Puccini-ish arias, magnificent ensembles, choruses of rude vigour, solemn and breathtaking spectacle, ravishing ballet music. There is a great deal of humour, and absolutely boundless exuberance.

The conception and composition of his first opera occupied Tippett for seven years (1946-52). It is a work which could never have been written to order. It sprang from the deepest inner sources, which made themselves available to Tippett, but belong to our collective unconscious. The initial impetus was a visual image whose apparition Tippett has vividly described:

> . . . in my mind's eye . . . I *saw* a stage picture (as opposed to hearing a musical sound) of a wooded hilltop with a temple, where a warm and soft young man was being rebuffed by a cold and hard young woman . . . to such a degree that the collective, magical archetypes take charge — Jung's *anima* and *animus* — the girl, inflated by the latter, rises through the stage flies to heaven, and the man, overwhelmed by the former, descends through the stage floor to hell. But it was clear they would soon return. For I saw the girl later descending in a costume reminiscent of the goddess Athena . . . and the man ascending in one reminiscent of the god Dionysus . . . (*Moving into Aquarius*)

In rendering this vision on stage Tippett was helped by memories of Bernard Shaw's *As Far As Thought Can Reach*, the fifth part of his 'metabiological pentateuch', *Back to Methuselah*. The setting of this part is 'a sunlit glade at the southern foot of a thickly wooded hill. On the west side of it, the steps and columned porch of a dainty little classic temple.' The time is 'summer afternoon in the year 31,920 A.D.' Youths and maidens dancing are interrupted by an Ancient who stumbles into them. One of the youths, Strephon, and his friend Chloe then discuss the meaning of youth and age with him, and she is inspired to assert a cold seniority over the ardent Strephon and leave him. Presently a She-Ancient appears. Then a human birth takes place out of an enormous egg. And so on.

These elements were adapted by Tippett in *The Midsummer Marriage* (except for the egg, whose literal employment he saved for his fourth opera,

The Ice Break, the new births in *The Midsummer Marriage* remaining figurative). The Greek temple, wooded hill, summer afternoon, dancing youths, Ancients, young couple who go apart, as well as the name of Strephon (allocated by Tippett to one of the dancer-neophytes of his Ancients), and the comedy's philosophy of enlightenment are all assimilated. So stark is the borrowing that one might say Tippett is actually setting Shaw to music (and arguably fulfilling the real and operatic potential of Shaw's art).

Tippett acknowledged another influence of Shaw on his evolving opera: 'But more to my purpose is Shaw's *Getting Married*, because the hindrances to the eventual marriage of that comedy are caused, if I remember right, by the prospective couple re-examining, on the wedding morning, themselves and their intentions in the light of some book of Shavian moral doctrine.' His young couple, Mark and Jenifer, have to undergo a process of ritual enlightenment before they can achieve the true marriage destined for them; and the doctrine they are serving is that previously uttered in Tippett's oratorio *A Child of Our Time*: 'I would know my shadow and my light,/ So shall I at last be whole.' Tippett once said that these lines make up 'the only truth I shall ever say' (TLS, July 8, 1977).

Tippett's metaphors for the enlightenment process draw not only on the rational, realistic, and science-fictional approaches of Shavian comedy, but on the magical and mythical means of such prototype operas as Mozart's *Die Zauberflöte* and Strauss's *Die Frau ohne Schatten*. The presence of a magical or supernatural world as it were *behind* the stage-set in an opera like Mozart's *Don Giovanni* or a play like Shakespeare's *A Midsummer Night's Dream* — a world to which only *some* of the realistic characters have access — greatly intrigued Tippett, who sought a similar 'stage of 'depth''. (MIA *ibid.*) The treatment of myth and the illusionism in T.S. Eliot's play *The Family Reunion* were also influential upon him.

After Shaw's influence, it is probably Eliot's that is the most important on the Tippett of *The Midsummer Marriage*, if not the Tippett of everything else. Tippett had hoped Eliot would write the text for *A Child of Our Time*; and though Eliot advised him to write it himself, he remained a valuable consultant on the problems of verse-theatre and music-drama. Not only do *The Midsummer Marriage*'s various allusions to Greek mythology echo those of *The Family Reunion* (in which 'realistic' drama, we recall, the Eumenides put in an appearance), but the opera can be read as a kind of optimistic commentary on, or even refutation of, Eliot's *The Waste Land*. The mythical, anthropological sources of the poem — Jessie L. Weston's *From Ritual to Romance*, Frazer's *The Golden Bough* — feed also into the opera. Two characters are virtually the same — the clairvoyante Sosostris and King Fisher (whose name inverts that of Eliot's mythic figure giving it a contemporary ring as in Duke Ellington or Shaw's Boss Mangan). There is a second young couple — Jack and Bella, mechanic and secretary — of prosaic disposition to contrast with the high-falutin' character of the other pair; and they make a connection with the low-life Eliot depicted in such *Waste Land* personnel as 'the typist home at teatime' and 'the young man carbuncle'. *The Waste Land* itself is referred to in one of Mark's arias; while Eliot's concluding *Fire Sermon* and its Buddhist philosophy inform Tippett's last act.

There are countless other literary and philosophical allusions in the libretto, which was universally deemed obscure at the time of the opera's first performance (1955), and has recently been found to cause few real problems. On the other hand, most of the early commentators never doubted the truth and effectiveness of the music. It was not only a huge lyrical expression unprecedented in music, but the more extraordinary for coming when it did: a joyful and life-giving English idyll:

at a time of world holocaust; and 'yet,' as Tippett said to an interviewer, 'it is not bland' (TLS *ibid.*). What has assured the work's success as a stage piece is not just the fact that the lineaments of its story and plot remain quite perceivable enough for traditional operatic purposes (*Il Trovatore*'s plot is much harder to follow), but the remarkable aptitude of this lyrical music as it unfolds to carry more and more, ultimately the whole, of the dramatic meaning.

*

The opera oozes with lyricism from its first page; but each stage-happening is precisely symbolized in musical terms. For instance, the manifestation of the Ancients' supernatural realm:

—an invention comparable to Mendelssohn's *Midsummer Night's Dream* flute chords, that fanfare at the gates of the fairyland. Or the Ancients' march out of the temple:

Whenever sunlight is mentioned the music subtly catches a major-key glint. When Jenifer ascends the mystical staircase her music soars luminously up with her (to a high B). Later when she reappears and descends, so the tremulous accompanying flute patterings take gradual downward steps. When 'stallions stamping' occur in Mark's description of his experiences underground, the accompaniment renders them in a flash.

The chorus has an enormously communicative role throughout the work; this is the choral opera *par excellence*. (Peter Gellhorn has compared it to a gigantic oratorio.) The choral writing varies between jubilant declamation, evocative intimation and supple madrigalianism. Each act ends with choral comment, the first unforgettably so (with a reprise of the vigorous semiquavers of the opening):

[4]

And by this stage in the opera one may feel that such musical surges are themselves what is convincingly moving the drama along. The collective force of myth and music are one.

Act Two bears out the feeling. It is almost all music; there are hardly any words. Three 'ritual dances' (originally referred to by the composer as 'racing dances') performed by Strephon and the other neophytes of the temple symbolize sexual, predatory and seasonal rhythms of nature. The hound

Jamie Cohen as Strephon in the 1983 American première in San Francisco (photo: William Acheson)

chases the hare (*The Earth in Autumn*); the otter hunts the fish (*The Waters in Winter*); the hawk preys upon the bird (*The Air in Spring*). The orchestral music Tippett has devised here is of extreme ductility, pictorialism and brilliance. It marks a new refinement in what might be called English impressionism; it is closer, that is, to the Ravel of *Daphnis and Chloe* (an analogy particularly fitting the sun-soaked music that fills the empty stage during the *Pre-Scene* of the act) than to anything by Bax.

But the music doesn't only serve an illustrative purpose; somehow it effects a deepening of the quest-drama in which Mark and Jenifer, though they remain invisible until the middle of Act Three, are currently involved. The other couple, Jack and Bella, witness the dances and gain from them their own, albeit less intense, enlightenment about the mysteries of *anima* and *animus*. Their charming, down-to-earth contributions — a discussion of marriage, a *chaleureux* lullaby:

[5]

and Bella's dewy song about make-up and hair-style — which frame the ballet music help to make, by force of contrast, a magical scene more so. In the *Post-Scene* the chorus passes briefly across the back of the hill, as it had done at the beginning of the act, and the stage is left empty again except for music.

The third act begins with some 'tipsyness, representative,' as Ian Kemp has written, 'of the imbalance prompted by psychic upheaval, and a piece of buffoonery, a natural response in the face of momentous revelation.' The buffoonery is a parody presentation by Jack of the clairvoyante (or '*mana* personality,' as Kemp refers to her) Sosostris, and the revelation her real subsequent utterance, a set-piece of uniquely Tippet-ian lyricism and emotive force. The text is based on a poem by Paul Valéry, *La Pythie*, in which a woman describes the loss of her womanhood and becoming a seer:

[6]

Out of this intensity an apparition of Mark and Jenifer in a lotus position symbolizing authentic union is produced. A fourth ritual dance, *Fire in Summer*, supervenes; and the music proliferates and convulses with even greater choral and orchestral splendour than hitherto. The drama of the opera has become a wholly musical epiphany; the music burns with an ecstatic, purifying fire. Even the new-dawn music at the end, initially and convincingly chilly and crisp, regains a final incandescence, as Jenifer and Mark and the chorus urge the truth of W.B. Yeats's poem *Lapis Lazuli*: 'All things fall and are built again,/ And those that build them again are gay.'

*

The exorbitant lyrical inspiration of *The Midsummer Marriage* proved good also for a number of contemporaneous 'satellite' works. The Concerto for Piano and Orchestra, the tenor and piano song-cycle, *The Heart's Assurance* (settings, to underline the paradox of *Midsummer Marriage*'s gestation, of World War Two poems about 'love under the shadow of death'), the orchestral *Suite for the Birthday of Prince Charles* (whose fourth movement quotes Ex. 3 above) and the string *Fantasia Concertante on a Theme of Corelli* all movingly echo that 'certain marvellous thing' Tippett had to say in his opera. And though its explosion of beautiful sound represents a significant development in Tippett's compositional technique, the opera maintains strong continuity, too, with his earlier works, even the relatively immature Sonata for Piano (1936-7, revised 1942), which resemblance is noticeable by playing the sonata and immediately afterwards the *Midsummer Marriage* piano score. The rhythmic experiments of the three earlier string quartets are consolidated in the opera, as are the explorations of madrigal technique in *The Source* and *The Windhover* (1942).

Tippett's musical style changed outwardly with the writing of his next opera *King Priam*, 1958-1961. But until then it could have been very broadly characterized as neo-classical, maintaining affiliations with the styles of Stravinsky and Hindemith. With Benjamin Britten's style it shared a common debt to Purcell more than anything else; and the similarities with other contemporary British music were fainter. (It is interesting that Arthur Bliss undertook an opera, *The Olympians*, to a libretto by J.B. Priestley, with subject matter uncannily close to Tippett's, at about the time *The Midsummer Marriage* was taking shape in its composer's mind. Tippett has often, apparently, benefited from such pre-emptive coincidences.)

There are many impressive features of the *Midsummer Marriage* style: its melding of modal, tonal and a 'modern' harmony built on the interval of a fourth, its rigorous and sinewy contrapuntal base, its felicities of phrasing,[15] its orchestration at once reedy and mellifluous, its propensity for musical onomatopoeia. But most impressive perhaps is its ability to combine neo-classical (more properly, neo-baroque) sectional structure and manner of 'stopping-and-starting' with the production of a gorgeous river of sound on which the voices can ride. The combination, not the two separate phenomena, is the crucial means by which this opera becomes music's and drama's most authentic and irresistible expression of ecstasy.

Note: The references in this article are to *Moving into Aquarius* (MIA); a *Times Literary Supplement* interview with Patrick Carnegy, July 8, 1977 (TLS); Peter Gellhorn in 'Tippett's Operas: A Musical Survey', *Composer*, Summer 1980; and 'The Dream Works of Michael Tippett', Ian Kemp, TLS, October 27, 1972.

The Midsummer Marriage

An Opera in Three Acts by Michael Tippett

Libretto by Michael Tippett

The Midsummer Marriage was first performed at The Royal Opera House, Covent Garden on January 27, 1955. The first performance in the United States was at the San Francisco Opera on October 15, 1984.

Note: the figures in square brackets refer back to Paul Driver's music examples. The footnotes to the libretto are a mixture of the composer's own notes and indications of where he has authorised cuts for performance. The small numbers in the libretto refer to John Lloyd Davies's textual notes, see pages 53-62.

Barbara Hepworth's design for the transfigured Mark and Jenifer in Act Three at Covent Garden, 1955

CHARACTERS

Mark *a young man of unknown parentage* tenor
Jenifer *his betrothed, a young girl* soprano
King Fisher *Jenifer's father, a business man* baritone
Bella *King Fisher's secretary* soprano
Jack *Bella's boy-friend, a mechanic* tenor
Sosostris *a clairvoyante* alto
The Ancients *Priest and Priestess of* { bass
 the Temple mezzo-soprano

Chorus of Mark's and Jenifer's friends
Strephon *one of the attendants*
Dancers *attendant on the Ancients*

Otakar Kraus as King Fisher in the world première at Covent Garden in 1955, produced by Christopher West, designed by Barbara Hepworth (photo: Houston Rogers, Theatre Museum)

26

Act One

Morning

Scene One. *Chorus. The scene is in twilight before day-break.* [1]

SEMI-CHORUS 1
(off, left)

This way! This way!
Don't go too far down there
But keep the path together.

Repeated nearer. Semi-Chorus 1 enters, left.

MEN

Here's a clearing in the wood.
Is this the place he meant?

GIRLS

I hope it gets lighter soon.
Anything might happen here.
What's that?

MEN

Only mist.
It will clear when the sun rises.
But where are all the rest?

SEMI-CHORUS 2
(off, right)

Hulloa! Hulloa!

SEMI-CHORUS 1
(all)

That must be them calling.

SEMI-CHORUS 2
(nearer)

Hulloa!

SEMI-CHORUS 1

Hulloa!

SEMI-CHORUS 2

Hulloa!

SEMI-CHORUS 1

We've found the place.
Come on. Come on.

SEMI-CHORUS 2
(entering right)

Thank heaven we've found you.

GIRLS (SEMI-CHORUS 2)

Whatever did we come for?

MEN (SEMI-CHORUS 2)

Where's Mark?

GIRLS (SEMI-CHORUS 2)

Where's Jenifer?

FULL CHORUS: MEN

Are you sure we've found the place?

FULL CHORUS: GIRLS

Oh, anything might happen here.

MEN

But look, it's nearly sunrise
And getting lighter.

The scene has been getting lighter. The sun rises.

ALL

The sun, the sun! Ah, midsummer morning!
Our spirits rise towards the bright
Comfort of the morning light.
The sun, the sun! Ah, midsummer morning!

The mist rises from the buildings.

GIRLS

Oh look — the temple there!

MEN

The meeting place that Mark appointed.

GIRLS

It seems much nearer than expected.

They look at the buildings for a moment in silence. Strange music off; flutes and bells. [2]

GIRLS

What's that?

MEN

Surely music?

GIRLS

I don't like it.

MEN

Listen, listen.

They listen. Music off, again.

GIRLS

Oh, I'm frightened.

MEN

Don't be frightened.

GIRLS

Someone's coming.

27

MEN

Let's hide away among the trees.

GIRLS

Yes, let's hide away among the trees.

ALL

Let's hide away among the trees.

They do so.

Scene Two. *Ancients, Dancers, later Mark. The dancers come from the temple led by Strephon playing a flute,[1] followed by the Ancients. A March. [3] On a signal from the He-Ancient the dancers execute a sword [or stick] dance. A dance. The dance ends with a clap of hands or sticks. Mark enters quickly.[2]*

MARK

Stop!

The Ancients pay no attention and order the dance a second time. Mark, after a moment's uncertainty, breaks up the dance.

MARK

Stop! Stop! Stop!

HE-ANCIENT

Young man, young man,
What right have you thus to break the
    dance?

MARK

I want a new dance for my wedding day.
Strange was my birth[3]
And strange my fate,
My wedding should be strange.
Is that not right?

HE-ANCIENT

Take care! A new dance
May well be strange but dangerous.

MARK

What nonsense!

SHE-ANCIENT

What impertinence!

MARK
(turning to the She-Ancient)

Look at your dancers then —
They are young like me.
        (to the dancers)
You want a new dance?

SHE-ANCIENT

Children, be still!

HE-ANCIENT

Change the unchanging ritual,
There'll be no point of rest —

SHE-ANCIENT

— No grace, no beauty.

MARK

Your words are vapours in the summer sun.
On this day, this day
Anything can happen
And everyone shall dance for me.

HE-ANCIENT

Then watch your new dance,
And you will see.

The He-Ancient orders the dance to begin again. Mark shows at first bewilderment and then exasperation that the dance is the same as before, until the He-Ancient, who has been moving around the dancers, suddenly trips Strephon, who falls to the ground with a crash.[4]

MARK

Monstrous! Monstrous!

Mark runs to Strephon.

Strephon, are you hurt?

He helps him up.

Can you walk?

Strephon tries to walk with Mark's help, and is received by the other dancers. Mark turns to the He-Ancient.

MARK
(passionately)

Oh, what a wicked thing to do,
Trying to break Strephon's leg.
Have you no sense of the proper care
For a dancer's trained body?

HE-ANCIENT

That is a lesson for *you* to learn,
Who think that change is only harmless —

SHE-ANCIENT

While it may sweep all trace of fragile
Beauty from its senseless path.

MARK

You twist my meaning, for you're envious
    of our youth.

HE-ANCIENT

No!
We do not desire your youth, nor seek
To hold you longer from your dreams.
You shall learn a new dance
Before you leave this place today.

The Ancients and the dancers return within the temple and the doors close behind them. March repeated.

28

Scene Three. *Mark, Chorus.*

CHORUS
(coming from behind the trees)[5]

O Mark, who are they?
Have you known them long?

MARK

I don't know who they really are,
But I've seen them since boyhood.

I've come here on summer nights
And mornings such as these.
Then is the temple nearer.
They are close, and if I wait
Eventually appear.

I call them the Ancients,
For they're so old, and never change.
I think they know the secret of my birth,
But will not tell me.

They'll come back, so let them be,
And turn to other things:
My marriage and my plan
To give the ring to Jenifer
Here in this magic wood
And on midsummer-day.
If no new dance,
At least new song to greet her.
For what can match the splendour of my
     pride
When she appears before you all as my
     bride?

Ah, ah[6] . . . the summer morning dances in
     my heart.
There, there's the lark ascending from the
     field.
No man is happier than I,
No woman lovelier than she,
And like the lark I sing for joy because I
     love —
I love, I love, I love, I love —
And like the lark I sing for joy because I love.

Jenifer enters. She is dressed for a journey.

Scene Four. *Mark, Jenifer, Chorus.*

MARK

Jenifer, Jenifer, my darling.
But — but — your dress?
Upon our wedding day?

JENIFER

Today there'll be no wedding.

MARK

No wedding! Why?

JENIFER

Why? Why have I come here,
Here when all the world's to choose?
This heat . . . this place . . .
No, no — I must go further,
Out of sound and out of sight.[7]

MARK
(echoing)

Out of sight? I see. You're frightened
Of your ranting father.

JENIFER

I've come away from him,
And left his home for good.

MARK

And hoping for a better home
You've come away to me, to me.

JENIFER

No. I must leave you, too.
I'll come back — perhaps — perhaps.

MARK

Jenifer, what, then don't you love me any
     more?

CHORUS
(sotto voce)

They're quarrelling.
Oh, what's the trouble?

JENIFER

It isn't love I want, but truth.

MARK

Truth?
See, see — the summer morning dances in
     my heart.

JENIFER

It isn't love I want, but truth.

MARK

Come now, kiss me and forget!

JENIFER

Don't touch me![8]

MARK

Are you mad?

JENIFER

Rudeness will not hold me either.
How can I break free from you all?
          (turning away upstage)
Where? Where?

CHORUS

They're quarrelling.
Oh, what's the trouble?

          Mark runs round in front of her.

MARK

Stop!
You shan't go!
I won't let you.

JENIFER

Out of my way!

29

Out of my way!

She walks by him and finds herself at the foot of the stone steps.

Now I know where I shall go.
(*turning down stage*)
What steps are those?

MARK
(*sotto voce*)

Those steps are broken.

JENIFER

This summer sun makes me see further.

Jenifer shades her eyes to look.

MARK

Surely you won't ascend them?
Jenifer, for pity's sake,
Don't go there.

JENIFER
(*with resolution*)

For me, the light!
For you, the shadow!
O magic staircase that I've always known
In dreams since childhood at my mother's knee,
At last, at last, I set my feet
Upon the way to heaven.
Up, up I climb to paradise.

She slowly climbs the stone steps.

GIRLS

Up, up she climbs to paradise.

MEN

The staircase has no end, she's bound to fall.

MARK
(*to the men*)

She's mad, she's mad.
(*to Jenifer*)
Come back, Jenifer,
Come back.
Ah —

Jenifer unexpectedly disappears from sight.

She's vanished in the light
And I am left in darkness.

GIRLS
(*laughing*)

Ha, ha, ha . . .

MEN

Come, Mark, don't grieve.
She'll come back.

GIRLS

Ha, ha, ha . . .

MARK

Oh, I am left in darkness.

KING FISHER
(*off, right*)

Hulloa! Hulloa!

GIRLS

King Fisher's voice!

MEN

Now, Mark, you can't stay here.

MARK

— in darkness.

KING FISHER

Hulloa! Hulloa!

GIRLS

He's surely coming after Jenifer.

MARK

— in darkness.

GIRLS
(*to the men*)

Oh, make Mark go away!

MEN

Mark, wake up! Wake up!
(*lifting him*)
Up, up, up!

MARK

— darkness.

MEN

Up, up, up!

MARK

Then let me go
To darkness as she told me.
(*with resolution*)
For her, the light!
For me, the shadow!
Gates I have always longed to enter,
Open to receive your child.

The gates fly open. Mark enters the cave and the gates crash to behind him. King Fisher rushes on in time to see them shut and Mark disappearing.

Scene Five. *King Fisher, Bella, Chorus, Ancients.*

MEN
(*laughing*)

Ho, ho, ho, ho . . .

KING FISHER
(*turning to the men*)

What are you laughing at?
It's no laughing matter

If my daughter's left me for a bastard.

After a moment he calls —

Bella, — Bella, — hurry here.
Hurry, hurry, hurry.

BELLA
(off)

Here I am.
Here . . .

She enters.

. . . I am.
(a little breathless)
I was coming as quick as I could.

KING FISHER

I've just seen Mark run away down there.

BELLA

Down there?

KING FISHER

Jenifer is surely with him too.

BELLA

You think she may be with him too?

KING FISHER
(looking around)

What sort of place is this, d'you think?

BELLA

It's rather odd for a house.
(to the Chorus)
Does anybody live here?

GIRLS

Very strange folk indeed.

MEN

By name the Ancients.

GIRLS
(ironic)

Their door is further up.

KING FISHER
(pompous)

Knock then, Bella, and enquire within.

Bella goes on to the upper stage.

BELLA

There's no knocker, but a kind of bell.

She rings a hanging bell. After a moment's expectation, the doors of the temple slowly open, and the Ancients come gravely through them and on to the upper stage. King Fisher goes down stage right and keeps his back turned to the Ancients.

SHE-ANCIENT

Who are you?
What do you want?

BELLA
(matter-of-fact and quickly)

I'm King Fisher's secretary.
He wants me to ask you about those gates.
He thinks his daughter may be down there.
Do you know if that is so?

SHE-ANCIENT

Where his daughter goes is her affair.

HE-ANCIENT

The gates are strange,
And only open for the proper people.

Bella goes down stage to where King Fisher is, and reports:

BELLA

They say the gates are strange,
And open only for the proper people.

KING FISHER

What riddling is that?
I fear they're not worth talking to,
But ask them who the proper people are.

Bella returns to the Ancients.

BELLA
(with pride)

The great King Fisher wants to know —

SHE-ANCIENT
(interrupting)

Should he not speak to us himself?
He's easily in hearing.

BELLA
(outraged)

That would never do.
He deals with everyone through me.
He only speaks, speaks
To people as important as himself.

HE-ANCIENT

Tell him there are no proper people here.

Bella goes again to King Fisher, and reports:

BELLA

They say the proper people are not here.

KING FISHER

What rigmarole! Tell them
We need the gates set open or I'll force them.

BELLA

I don't think they'll consent to that.

KING FISHER

Then we'll proceed without consent.

He dismisses her. Bella turns to go. The Ancients have returned into the temple.

BELLA

Oh! They're gone!
How very odd.

KING FISHER
(*turning round*)

That's no behaviour fit for me.
I'll not forget. — And now?

BELLA

Perhaps you'll have to force the gates,
Though they will certainly object.

KING FISHER

Who's to do that?

BELLA

Well, there's Jack.

KING FISHER

Who's Jack?

BELLA

Oh — he's a honey.

KING FISHER

A what?

BELLA

I mean a workman — a mechanic.

KING FISHER

Then Jack's the man for me.
Go. Go. Fetch him at once.

BELLA

But —

KING FISHER

Go. Go. No more delay. Go.
Bella goes.
I'll keep watch till you return.

Scene Six. *King Fisher, Chorus.*

KING FISHER
(*turning to the men*)

So you, so you — are Mark's fine brood of
   friends.
But he's a ne'er-do-well, a ne'er-do-well,
A loafer sponging on the state,
Whom you presume to emulate
This summer morning.

Do not be misled, my boys,
Mark's a tempter and a rascal,
Stealing your hearts away from work
And duty you so gladly shirk
This summer morning.

While I, King Fisher, I, the clever business
   man,
Trying by all the means I know
To guard the honour of my daughter,

I've some work for you:
(*pointing left*)
To spy that way behind that wall,
To see what dangers to expect.
What! You shy away.
Where's your sense of courage and
   adventure?
Will that not spur you?
Will that not spur you?
Then I'll call the tune.
You fancy people may despise me,
But look — here's money!

   He takes a purse from his pocket.

Don't you like it?

*He holds up a coin and waves it before
them.*

Don't you want it?
Here! Catch, catch.
Catch if you can.

   He throws the coin to the men.

CHORUS (MEN)

Here! Catch, catch.
Catch if you can.

KING FISHER
(*interrupting*)

Now, you boys, it's time to start
To do the work you're paid for,
So let me see you go.
That way! That way!
The sooner the going
The quicker return,
The quicker return,
And remember, you fellows, remember,
Don't dally around,
Swimming in streams
So gay in the sun there
High in the heavens
Already at noon,
For I am the boss now,
And pay for you.

*King Fisher drives the men off left, and
turns to the girls.*

So you, so you — so you're the company
   my daughter keeps.
But she's her head in air, her head in air,
In cloud cuckoo-land — 'twas child's play
For Mark to make her run away
This summer morning.

Do not be beguiled, my dears,
For I, King Fisher, I, a loving, generous
   father,
Hoping to show you, if I can,
The real way to help my daughter,
I've some work for you:
(*pointing right*)
To spy that way behind that wall
To see what dangers to expect.
You shy away.

Where's your sense of pity and devotion?
Will that not move you?
You fancy people may despise me,
But look — here's money!

He takes a purse again from his pocket.

Don't you like it?
Don't you want it?

*He takes out a coin as before and prepares to
throw it to the girls, but before he can do so
they recoil.*

CHORUS (GIRLS)

No! No!

KING FISHER

What?

CHORUS (GIRLS)

No!

KING FISHER

What?

CHORUS (GIRLS)

No!
Whatever you offer,
No truck with a bribe,
No truck with a bribe.

KING FISHER
(*furious*)

Are you crack-pots,
Or very high-minded,
Refusing a wage
Paid for the work
That's got to be done?
Well, boggle at money,
You'll do it without,
For I am the King here.
Be off with you!

He drives the girls off, right, and is left alone.

Scene Seven. *King Fisher, Jack, Bella,
later Chorus. Enter Bella with Jack. He is in
overalls.*

JACK

Here I am, Sir,
What can I do?

KING FISHER

I want the gates there opened.
Do it promptly. I'll pay you well.

Jack goes to try the gates again.

JACK

They're firmly shut. But sure
We'll have them open in a moment.

He comes back to look in his bag for a tool.

BELLA

Should we not ask the owners if they mind?

KING FISHER

No!
You spoke with them yourself and know it's
useless.

Jack goes to try the gates again.

BELLA

But *do* be careful, Jack, you know
I'm worried by the people here.

JACK

But even if you are,
What can I do?

KING FISHER

Take no notice! No.

JACK

No.

KING FISHER AND JACK

A job's a job, and there's no question,
A working man must do as told,
And trust the one who pays him, for
A job's a job and there's no question.

Jack prepares the tools he is to use.

JACK

Like every working man I know
How best to do my single job.
My card will tell you who I am
And what the weekly wage I earn.
But it can't tell you what I dream.

BELLA

Ah, Jack!

JACK

That's only known to *me* —

BELLA

Ah, Jack!

JACK

To *me* — and you.

BELLA

Ah!

BELLA AND JACK

Ah, ah,
Life's dull until our work is over,
When you and I walk out together,
Down the roadway courting, for
Life's dull until our work is over.

They dance and embrace.

KING FISHER
(*interrupting*)
Just come along, you two, and hurry.
Your working hours aren't over yet.

33

JACK

Very well then, I'll begin.

He lifts a hammer to do so.

VOICE OF SOSOSTRIS
(*apparently from within the gates*)[9]

Take care,
King Fisher.
A well-wisher
Says: Beware!

BELLA
(*anxiously*)

Whatever's that?
I knew for certain
They'd be offended.

CHORUS (GIRLS)
(*off stage*)

Stop!

They enter right.

Stop, oh stop, King Fisher, now
We know it's wrong to tamper with the
gates.
Stop, we implore you!
Tell Jack, your man who's standing by
them now,
To stop!

BELLA

There, Jack, you see
They think as I do — as I do.

JACK

But, Bella, they're being frightened by a
voice.
That's all, a voice.

BELLA

No, Jack, no, they think as I do . . .

KING FISHER
(*shouting*)

Quiet! Quiet!
Be quiet all of you, don't babble.
Nothing's there to be afraid of.
Go on, Jack, go on, Jack,
I'll answer for you.

JACK

Very well, I'll try again.

He does so.

VOICE OF SOSOSTRIS
(*apparently from within the gates*)

Take great care,
Proud King Fisher.
A true well-wisher
Says again: Beware!

BELLA

The warning voice again.

Oh dear, it's certain
They've been offended.

GIRLS

Ah . . .

MEN
(*off stage*)

On!

They enter left.

On, go on, King Fisher, now
We know the voice is nothing but a trick.
Go on, we advise you.
Make Jack, your man, who's standing by
the gates,
Go on.

JACK

There, Bella, there,
What did I tell you?

BELLA

Don't listen to them, Jack,
They're quite mistaken.

JACK

But Bella, but Bella,
Surely they're saying what they know?
But surely you're being frightened by a
voice
That's all a trick.

BELLA

Don't listen to them, Jack,
They're quite mistaken,
But *they*, they think as I do . . .

GIRLS

Stop, oh stop . . .

MEN

Go on, go on we exhort you,
Make Jack, your man, who's standing by
the gates,
Go on.

KING FISHER
(*shouting*)

Oh, but my patience is exhausted.
What do you take me for, a fool?
There'll be no further stalling at the labour
you've undertaken.
So:
(*storming*)
Go on, go on, for I'm your master.

BELLA

Dear Jack, I'm frightened now.
Do leave it.

KING FISHER

Go on, for I'm your master.

JACK

Then I've no choice,
But I don't like it.

CHORUS (MEN)

We know it's but a game to trick us
In hopes to see us go.

CHORUS (GIRLS)

We know he'd better leave the gates
That shut the path to hell.

BELLA
(to Jack)

Why must all this rest on you
To make so terrible a move?

KING FISHER
(to Jack)

Why be frightened by a voice
While I am there to stand beside you?

MEN

Jack should pay no further heed to Bella's
    womanish misgivings . . .

GIRLS

Jack won't pay sufficient heed to Bella's
    sibylline misgivings . . .

BELLA

Dear Jack, I'm frightened now.
Do leave it in some other hands than yours.

KING FISHER

Go on, go on, for I'm your master
Who intends a duty to be done.

MEN

Will King Fisher be deterred by a mere
    voice
Within the gates?
Shake the whole earth with the sound of
    our shout:
Go on!

GIRLS

Then where can we now turn for aid
In this extremity of apprehension?
Lift up your voices to the heavens, and cry:
    Help!

MEN

Shake the whole earth with the sound of
    our shout: Go on!

GIRLS

Lift up your voices to the heavens, and cry:
    Help!

KING FISHER

Hear your master who commands you to
    obey.
Hear your master who commands you to
    proceed.

BELLA

Trust your sweetheart who sees clearly.
Trust your sweetheart who knows best.

Scene Eight. / *Finale. King Fisher, Chorus, Jenifer, later Mark, Ancients, Dancers. Jenifer appears at the top of the steps, in white, partially transfigured.*[*10] *Jack and Bella slip away.*

GIRLS

Jenifer!

MEN

Jenifer!

KING FISHER

My daughter, Jenifer!

JENIFER
She slowly descends to the bottom.

Returning to the earth is cruel.
Here you are never still nor calm.

KING FISHER

Don't give yourself such airs, young lady.
It's a wonder you are not with Mark.

JENIFER

A very gracious heavenly wonder
That makes him infinitely far away.

KING FISHER

He's safely far away down there,
So surely now's the proper time
To leave him?
Come now with me
And drop this childish masquerade.

JENIFER

Am I not masked before my earthly father?
Now is too late to run from Mark.
My return makes him return.

The gates open. Mark appears in the gates' mouth in red, partially transfigured.† *He*

---

* The ancient Greek prototype towards which Jenifer's transfiguration is tending would be Athena. (Athena was born without mother from Zeus's head.) No exact imitation of Athena is meant, for the natural Jenifer is still visible behind the supernatural transformation.

†The ancient Greek prototype towards which Mark's transfiguration is tending would be Dionysus. (Dionysus, son of earth-born Semele, had a second birth from Zeus's thigh.) No exact imitation of Dionysus is meant, for the natural Mark is still visible behind the supernatural transformation.

shades his eyes against the light and stands thus for some time.

MARK

Returning to the light is cruel.
Here you are ever calm and dull.
(*passionately*)
Beats not my body to the wine-red blood?[11]

JENIFER

Flies not my spirit to the swan-white sky?
Singing: I am a child of the starry heaven.

MARK

Shouting: I am a child of the fruitful earth.[12]

JENIFER

— of the starry heaven.

MARK

— of the fruitful earth.

JENIFER

— of heaven.

MARK

— of earth.

JENIFER

— of heaven.

MARK

— of . . .

Fanfare. The temple doors open and the Ancients come out with the dancers.

HE-ANCIENT

Prepare to justify your strife.
Let the girl speak first.

SHE-ANCIENT
(*coming forward between Mark and Jenifer*)

See no hint of spiritual pride
Mar the contest that you now begin.
Pride has subtle and peculiar power
To swell the stomach but not heal the heart.
You are contained within the spirit,
Not the spirit shrunk in you,
Else it burst the bonds and break you.

She returns up stage. The girl dancers have now taken position near Jenifer.

JENIFER

Is it so strange if I resent
The fatal pressure from the world around me,
Denying life to my poor straitened soul?

For her sake, then, with clear intent
Leaving the home, I thrust my lover from me,
To climb the staircase to my heavenly goal.

A girl dancer climbs the steps behind Jenifer to blow upon a silver trumpet.

Sweet was the peace,
Joyful the calm.
Strong was the light,
Cleansing the air.

> *The girl dancers move to the music.*

Then the congregation of the stars began
To dance: while I in pure delight
Saw how my soul flowered at the sight
And leaving the body forward ran
To dance as well. How can I
Such lovely visions of the mind deny?

The girls of the Chorus begin to move with the dancers and try to get nearer Jenifer.

GIRLS

Teach us, Jenifer, to rise
Above our cares into the skies.

KING FISHER
(*interrupting, and trying to reach Jenifer through the girls and the girl dancers*)

We live on earth and not in heaven,
Nor is there disgrace in that.
Common folk have common cares
And common duties to their state.
So —

HE-ANCIENT
(*interrupting*)

All comment is clearly out of place
While judgment is suspended for the half.
Therefore stand back! It is the other's turn.

The men dancers have taken position near Mark, driving King Fisher once more down stage.

MARK
(*to the men of the Chorus*)

You, you who were with me when she left me,
How did the lover look when she had gone?

MEN

A crestfallen cock,
A crumpled child
Crying: darkness.

MARK

Then, when you had lifted me against my will,
What outer darkness answered to my own?[13]

MEN

A deeper dark[14]
Disclosed abruptly
In the hill-side hidden.

MARK

When I passed the gate of horn,[15]
What happened then, reading the riddle right?

36

MEN

How could we see behind the bars,
No summer sunshine following in?

*A man dancer ascends the hillside behind
Mark to clash later a pair of bronze cymbals.*

MARK

Down, downwards to the centre,[16]
Doubled downwards,
Crawling, falling,
Rocked in a boat across the water[17]
Coldly lapping
The waste land
To thread the labyrinthine maze
Of fear that guards the lovely meadows.

MEN

That is no song to rouse our tired
Hearts and steel our lazy limbs.

*The cymbals clash. The men dancers move
to the music.*[18]

MARK

As stallions stamping
The young men dance
To the springing sap
And the leaping life.

We force our feet through the great grass
And tear the boughs from the bending trees[19]
That hold the sun from the glorious bed
Where she, lying fallow through the winter,
Slept, till pricked awake by our desire.

MEN

*(beginning to be fascinated by the singing and
the dancing)*

This music rises as the spring tides
Rise to overflow before they ebb.

MARK

As stallions stamping
The young men dance
To the springing sap
And the leaping life.

The ewe is torn by our willing hands,
The child trod by our frenzied feet[20]
That beat the beat of life inflamed[21]
By death. There is no union but in full
Communion, Man with Beast and All in
One.

*The men of the Chorus begin to move with
the dancers, and try to get nearer to Mark.*

MEN

Show us, Mark, another birth
As common children of the earth.

JENIFER
(taking a step forward)

Ah, but the price for that, the price?

MEN

The price?

JENIFER

See by a heavenly magic in this glass[22]
The fearful face behind the mask.

*She moves slowly and triumphantly across
the stage towards Mark.*

Look as I bring it near you, look,
Mark, that you may see the truth.
Are you so easy shamed to turn aside?
(exultant)
Ah, what a triumph for the right!

MARK

Did I not learn a magic too
From all that happened in the cave?
Here I take this golden branch[23]
Whose vital virtue now lets me
Turn in power. Jenifer,
Prepare to see your mirror — fall.

*He turns and the glass falls from Jenifer's
hands.*

JENIFER

Oh — what an evil devil's stroke!
Malefic magic and perverted power.
Are you a serpent, I become a saint?
Then am I Mark, and go to find the beast.[24]

*She enters the gates, her dress catching the
reflection of a red glow. The gates close
behind her. During the next music, Mark
crosses to the steps and slowly climbs them,
his dress catching the reflection of a white
light. He goes out of sight. The Ancients and
dancers go into the temple.*

KING FISHER

Now is this nonsense at its noon.
But I'll be even with it yet.
(to the girls)
Jenifer has lost her senses utterly,
Possessed by this midsummer madness.

CHORUS (GIRLS)

Joan heard the voice first[25]
In father's garden at high noon,
The summer sun prefiguring the flame.

KING FISHER
(to the men)

Mark shall go down and fetch her back,
And then, perhaps, I'll give him leave to
marry.

CHORUS (MEN)

Mark has no ear for you, King Fisher,
Climbing his path from hell to heaven.[26]
No promise, nor the threat
Of violence will hold him now.

KING FISHER

But mark my words, the insulting boy
Will come to heel and whimper in the end.

*He goes off, as the Chorus join together and
wheel down to the front of the stage.*

CHORUS (FULL)

Let Mark and Jenifer endure for us
The perils of the royal way,
We are the laughing children.[27]

    They laugh.   [4]

We are the laughing children.
Free, fresh, fine,
Strong, straight, stark,
Rough, raw, rude,
Gallant, grim and gay.

    Curtain.

*Peter Massocchi as He-Ancient and Maureen Guy as She-Ancient in the 1976 Welsh
National Opera production, produced by Ian Watt-Smith (photo: Julian Sheppard)*

Act Two

Afternoon

The stage set is turned slightly to the right, so that the stone steps have gone out of sight and only the doors and the left-hand corner of the temple are visible, slantwise across the right of the stage. The gates are now left-centre, with more of the wood and hillside in view to the further left.

Pre-Scene. *Strephon, Chorus off stage. Strephon is discovered standing motionless on the corner of the temple steps, listening. After a while, Strephon relaxes his pose and begins to dance down centre. He stops, hesitates, then runs off behind the temple, as the Chorus is heard singing in the distance. The Chorus's song comes nearer.*

CHORUS
(off stage)

In the summer season on the longest day of all,
We wander through the woods where the cunning cuckoos call,
Crying as they're flying, and this is what they say:
She must leap and he must fall[28]
When the bright sun shines on midsummer-day.

Scene One. *Bella, Jack, Semi-Chorus (Full-Chorus off stage). Bella enters left, with Jack behind her. A section of the Chorus follows. The rest of the Chorus continue on their way, moving off stage from left to right, and singing their song repeatedly.*

BELLA
(drawing Jack down stage away from the Semi-Chorus)[29]

Jack, don't let's go with all the others,
Stay behind a bit with me.
I've something for your ear alone.

SEMI-CHORUS (GIRLS)

Where are you two going?
Aren't you coming with us to play games?

SEMI-CHORUS (MEN)

Perhaps they've games of their own to play!

They all laugh.

GIRLS

Let them go or we shall lose the others.

They turn to go.

MEN

That's true.

CHORUS (ALL)

Bye, bye.
In the summer season on the longest day of all . . .

They go back off stage after the others. Their voices disappear too into the distance.

JACK

They've gone now, Bella;
What is for my ear alone?

BELLA

I think you ought to guess.
That shouldn't be so hard.

JACK

I know you've always something new in mind.
But I can never guess.

BELLA

Oh! This time is quite different.
What day is it?

JACK

Midsummer-day.

BELLA

Isn't that excuse enough?

JACK
(with good humoured patience)

I've no idea.

BELLA

Oh! Jack, Jack!
Is it leap-year?

JACK
(less patiently)

You know the answer, Bella.
Why ask me?

BELLA

I feel as though it should be.
For Jack, you see, I've made my mind up.
It's time we married.

JACK

But Bella, I thought you —

BELLA
(interrupting)

Ah, that's past and gone.
We're going to marry now and settle.
Aren't you pleased?

39

JACK

Indeed I am!
Only the first shock of your decision.
So many problems rush to mind.

BELLA

Which you, the handyman, will solve.
While I, so far, have only one thing clear.
We're going to marry, settle down and have
  a home.
Agreed?

JACK

Agreed.

BELLA

If there's a little house to rent,
A girl can live her proper life.

JACK

A man in love was never meant
To wait for ever for his wife.

BELLA

And so as girl —

JACK

— and man —

BELLA

We come —

JACK

— together —

BELLA

— in our home.[30]

BOTH

And then —

BELLA

While you're at work I'll mind the place
And wash the clothes and cook the food.

JACK

And I'll work overtime in case
We need more money in the purse.

BELLA

For soon —

JACK

— there'll be —

BELLA

— a little Jack —

JACK

— or little Bella.

BELLA

Who can tell?

BOTH

And then —

BELLA   [5]

I'll lay the baby to my breast
And rock it, rock it gently in my arms:
Sleep, sleep, pretty little one, sleep.

JACK

And when the baby's quiet
I'll lift you on to my knee
And rock you, rock you to
Sleep, sleep, pretty little one, sleep.

BOTH

Sleep, sleep, pretty little one, sleep.

They kiss.

BELLA

Come within the shadow of the wood.

They get up and begin to move slowly across the stage. They stop and kiss again.

JACK

We'll go within the shadow of the wood.

They walk together slowly as in a dream across the stage into the wood left.

Scene Two. *Strephon, Dancers. Strephon enters from behind the temple. He goes to the corner of the temple steps, and takes up there the same pose as in the pre-scene. Once again after a while he relaxes his pose and begins to dance lightly down stage. Strephon ends his dance down stage centre in an attitude of expectation, to the music of bells and flutes. Some of the trees appear to move.[31] They move again. It is the other dancers who, breaking loose from their tree shapes begin to move freely about the stage. Strephon goes off stage behind the temple.*

The remaining dancers gaily mark the first racing course, for the first dance, with themselves as trees. The course is a roughly circular field with trees on the perimeter and one in the centre. When the course is set, the fact is announced by a flourish. The dancers stiffen into the roots of great trees, whose branches seem to disappear into the flies.

The Hare (Strephon) enters from the right on the upper stage beside the temple, and takes his place there, crouching at the root of one of the trees. At the same time, the Hound (the girl dancer) enters, down on the lower stage, and takes her place there, waiting.[32]

The First Dance — The Earth in Autumn

The Hound begins to hunt the Hare by scent, moving across the front of the stage from left to right. The Hound, getting warmer on the scent, begins to mount the steps to the upper stage. Here, at last, she gets the full scent, but is uncertain of the direction.

The Hare suddenly flies off, descending to the lower stage, and begins to run the course anti-clockwise, starting up stage. He moves in and out of the trees on the perimeter. The Hound chases after the Hare, but still mainly by scent. Twice the Hare is nearly caught, but on the third occasion when it looks as if capture were inevitable, the Hare does a double turn round the central tree, escapes, and runs off right. Here he is for a moment jubilant before going off the upper stage behind the temple.

In a dazzle of sunlight, the dancers come loose from the tree roots, and the trees themselves disappear. The Hound has gone off left.

The dancers move about again freely. They begin to mark the second course, for the second dance, always with themselves as trees. The course is a river, with trees on the banks, flowing diagonally across the stage down from the place where the temple steps end, right centre, to the left footlights. As before, the completion of the operation is marked by a flourish. The dancers stiffen into the roots of trees as before.

The Fish (Strephon) enters from the right on the upper stage, but near the footlights. He slides into his place, at the top of the river, sheltered by a tree root. At the same time, the Otter (a girl dancer) enters from the left upstage, and takes her place on the bank of the river, opposite the Fish.

The Second Dance — The Waters in Winter

The river begins to flow. The flow is visible where, down stage left, the water seems to eddy in the sunlight. The eddies have the form of water nymphs.

The Fish suddenly makes for the surface of the river to breathe, or catch flies. His direction is down stage. The Otter dives into the river. The Fish flashes back to the safety of the bank, sheltering under a tree root further down the river on the same side. The Otter swims about and whips up the waters in her anger. She climbs out of the river opposite the Fish. The commotion subsides. The eddies become noticeable again in the sunlight.

Once more, the Fish darts, and the Otter plunges after him. The Fish regains the bank further down on the same side, but the Otter climbs out on the same side of the river as the Fish, though further down. The commotion subsides once more. The eddies are visible again, but the air is troubled.

The Fish makes a dash, attempting to get past the Otter, who dives after him, pinning him against the further bank. The Fish gets entangled with the water nymphs, seeking to force himself through crannies too small for the Otter to pass. He seems to get stuck in one, and only escapes with a wrench. He goes off right onto the upper stage, but this time his jubilation is marred by the pain due to the wrench. He goes off stage right behind the temple.

In a dazzle of sunlight the dancers get loose from the tree roots and the river disappears. The Otter has gone off stage left.

The dancers sow a field of spring corn, moving right across the stage and returning. They begin to dance in ever smaller circles, gradually spinning into a group which finally comes to rest up stage right. The dancers now form a compact group of young trees.

The Third Dance — The Air in Spring

The leaves of the trees wave in the spring breeze. The Bird (Strephon) hops on to the stage from down stage right. The waving of the tree leaves is subdued. The Bird hops into the cornfield. He pecks at the grain. He hops on. He pecks again. He hops farther. The tree leaves begin a spring dance, which increasingly attracts the Bird's attention, as though his nest and mate were in the trees. He attempts to fly, but as one of his wings is broken, he falls at once to the ground. He is quickly up again and tries to fly once more. He falls again, heaves and so stays still. The shadow of the Hawk (a girl dancer) is thrown on to the stage, growing ever larger as she descends. The Bird hops under the protection of the trees. The Hawk turns back without becoming visible and her shadow diminishes and vanishes.

Once more the tree leaves resume their waving in the spring breeze, and the Bird hops out again after the grain. Once more he tries to carry grain into the trees, but when he flies, he falls again. The shadow of the Hawk descending is again projected on the stage, growing ever larger. The Bird with difficulty reaches the shelter of the trees. The Hawk appears and seems to hover on the cornice of the temple just long enough for the audience to see that it is a girl dancer with a bird mask and huge wings. She appears to fly away, her shadow diminishing again to nothing. nothing.

The tree leaves resume their waving for the third time. The Bird hurries out to peck the grain in such a frenzy that he pays no attention to the tree leaves' spring dance. However, he makes one last attempt to fly, but falls utterly exhausted. He does not move when the Hawk descends. The stage darkens nearly to black-out.

Bella, who, with Jack, has been watching this dance with increasing fascination and horror, screams, not knowing if what she sees is real or her own dreams. Strephon and the dancers vanish.

BELLA

Ah! They'll kill him!
(*clinging to Jack*)
Take me away. Take me away.
I can't bear it.[33]

On the verge of hysterics she buries her head in his arms. The stage darkness lifts in a dazzle of sunlight. The dancers having returned whence they came, the stage looks exactly the same as at the beginning of the Act.

JACK

There, Bella, steady, steady.
It's all right. I'm here.
They've gone now anyway.
I wonder who they were.

BELLA
(*half crying*)

I don't care who they were.
It's uncanny and unnatural.
I'm sure they meant to kill him.

JACK

Nonsense, Bella, that was only play.
You're still a-tremble.
I've never known you so upset.
You're always sure and strong.

BELLA
(*lifting her head, sadly*)

I wasn't born for all these mysteries.

She looks over Jack's shoulder; with returning gaiety.

Yes, they've gone.

JACK

That's the Bella that I know.
That's the voice I'm used to.
Let's go together now and find our friends.

BELLA

First let me look then in my glass.

She takes it from her pocket or her bag and looks at herself in it.

Oh — my face, my nose, my hair!
Hold the glass now, then you'll see
How the real Bella's made.[34]

They say a woman's glory is her hair.
(But only if it's properly displayed!)
Is it tangled?
Then we comb it,
Some to this side,
Some to that.
After, plait the strands together,
(Many a man's been caught for good,
Caught for good in a girl's hair.)
Weave the strands together till we
Can with skilful nimble fingers curl them
Up and pin them alluringly round the head.

Turn the glass a little, dear Jack, the way I
  need it.

They say a woman's fortune is her face.
(But only when it's given proper care!)
Is it pallid?
Then we paint it,
Some on this cheek,
Some on that.
After rouge the lips with carmine,

She hums the tune as she paints her lips.

Line the lips with carmine till we
Can with deftly subtle touches of the
  powder-
Puff, finish the enchantingly attractive face.

Take a new look at me!

She turns herself round and Jack admires her.

You see, I'm quite myself again,
Neat and ready to rejoin King Fisher.

JACK
(*recoiling*)

King Fisher?

BELLA

Oh, yes. He's summoned both of us.
You've another role to play.

JACK

Another role to play? For him?
What does King Fisher matter now?

BELLA

Jack, dear, our love has spoken.
Our home is sure.
I'll leave King Fisher at the proper time.
Today he's still my master,
And worth our while to suffer.

JACK
(*recoiling further*)

Now I have strange misgivings,
Unfriendly fancies and forebodings . . .

BELLA

Don't *you* go silly now.
Our world is fact not fancy,
And it's a fact that if you want to keep me
Catch me if you can, if you can.

She runs off left.

JACK
(*running after her*)

Bella, Bella . . .

42

Post-Scene. *Chorus off stage. The Chorus passes behind the hill, returning from right to left. The stage remains empty.*

CHORUS
(off stage)

In the summer season on the longest day of all,
We wander through the woods where the cunning cuckoos call,

Crying as they're flying, and this is what they say:
She must leap and he must fall
When the bright sun shines on midsummer-day.

The singing dies away in the distance. The presences are still.

Curtain.

Ragnhild Nordesjö as Sosostris at the Swedish première in Stockholm on February 8, 1982 (photo: Karl Gabor)

43

Act Three

Evening and Night

The scene has taken the necessary turn back to the left from what it was in Act Two, so that it is now the same as in Act One. That is, the temple is once again back centre, the stone staircase to the right, the gates and the cave to the left, and the steps leading from the upper to the lower stage in the appropriate place. When the curtain rises, the larger portion of the Chorus is singing and drinking after a meal on the left of the stage. But it is not clear at first glance what object they are surrounding or what they are laughing at.

Scene One. *Chorus.*

CHORUS

O-hay! O-hay![35]
At sundown
Celebrate the day's end
With bread, the fishes and the wine.

They laugh. On the right of the stage a small group is dancing to the sound of a fiddle. There is a fresh outburst from the group drinking.[36]

O-hay! O-hay!
At sundown
Celebrate the day's end
With bread, the fishes and the wine.

They laugh. The group spreads out and it becomes possible to see that they have given so much wine to one man that he is on the way to being tipsy.

Bread and fishes are the food
And wine the drink of men and gods.
And man is a god (so he thinks)[37]
When he's drunk too much!

They laugh heartily. The half-tipsy man lurches towards the group that's dancing.[38]

HALF-TIPSY MAN

Shall I dance you a fandango,
Boston, rumba or a tango?
I can step as light as any
Of you dainty dancers.

A DANCING MAN

Mind out, you fool!
Look where you're going.
Are you blind, are you drunk?

The tipsy man gets caught up in the dance. There is general laughter and the dance is given up. Everyone sings.

CHORUS

For bread
(When the yellow corn is ground)
Is but plain, and fish
(When the nets return from the blue sea)
    but homely fare.
But wine's pressed out from the ripened
    grape
In a red, rich juice for our delight,
For our delight (or our damnation)
When the midsummer sun goes down,
Down the long tunnel to the east
And the moon at the full[39], the White
    Goddess, starts
Her airborne journey to the west at night.

GIRLS

What does the night hold for us?

MEN

Her night or his night?
King Fisher summoned us tonight.

GIRLS

What does the Goddess ask or bring
But two things: love or death?

MEN

Surely King Fisher did not summon us for
    love?

GIRLS

Has he then summoned us for death?

Scene Two. *King Fisher, Bella, Chorus. King Fisher enters up stage quickly, with Bella, who carries a belt and a holster.*

KING FISHER

No! King Fisher summons you for victory!
    (*to Bella*)
Hang the holster on that tree in case of need.[40]
    (*to the world at large*)
These Ancients think that they're alone
In having access to the other world.
But that's not so.
I'll show them. I'll out-magic them.
I've called my private clairvoyante
And she'll unravel all their mysteries.
(*turning to the Chorus and striking an attitude*)
Go down and meet Madame Sosostris,
Greet her with song and lead her
Up with honours suited to a queen.

CHORUS

O-hay! O-hay! King Fisher, yes.
(*mimicking King Fisher's attitude*)
We'll go to meet Madame Sosostris,
Greet her with song and lead her
Up with honours suited to a queen.
O-hay! O-hay!

They stop attitudinising and go out laughing.

Scene Three. *King Fisher, Bella, Ancients.*

KING FISHER

Now, Bella, call the Ancients.

BELLA

Surely you're not wanting them again.

KING FISHER

Indeed, why not?
Please ring at once.

Bella, with less assurance than in the morning, does so. The doors of the temple open and the Ancients appear.

SHE-ANCIENT

What is the matter now?

BELLA

King Fisher wants to speak with you.

SHE-ANCIENT

If that is so, we're all attention.

KING FISHER

You two thought to have the better of me,
Catching my daughter in your trap like that.
I'm not the man to fall so easily.
I've sent for one who'll see through all your
schemes
To hold my daughter from her home.

HE-ANCIENT

She is in bondage to her fate, not us.

KING FISHER

Read me no riddles, for I'm in earnest.
Since you are obdurate
Receive my challenge
To a contest between power and power.
The prize is worthy. It's my daughter.
Defend yourselves!
For conjure what spirits that you may,
Sosostris will outwit you
Though the means be death.*

HE-ANCIENT

Truly his pride is riding a high
Mare intent to throw him for a fall.

SHE-ANCIENT

Truly the lure of fruit that hangs
Forbidden draws him blinded to his fate.

BELLA
(*aside*)

Truly I wish that Jack at last
Were here to pour an oil upon this fume.

KING FISHER
(*aside*)

Truly they know they're cornered and have
lost
The game before the starting whistle's
blown.

HE-ANCIENT
(*coming down towards King Fisher*)

King Fisher, I must give you warning.[41]
You meddle with powers you cannot gauge,
Courting a risk you do not understand.
Should you persist, there's mortal danger
To your person, and I tell you now:
Withdraw your challenge while you may.

KING FISHER
(*histrionically*)

And even if there's danger to my person,
What matters that before my daughter's
danger?
And should I further fall and go to ground
Before the violence of a stronger power,
Is that no honourable role to play?

SHE-ANCIENT

He shows a certain courage of his own.

KING FISHER

That may be so.
But the point at issue:
Do you accept my challenge?

HE-ANCIENT

Lifted to such lofty heights, I do.

Scene Four. *King Fisher, Bella, Ancients, Chorus and Jack.*

MEN

See! Where
We carry on our mighty shoulder
The Sphinx and the Sibyl rolled in one.

They enter carrying in procession a figure as though enthroned, dressed in a green cloak and conical hat, masked, or holding a crystal bowl in front of its face. Behind the figure as it comes down centre, members of the Chorus raise flags and banners [or branches] so that temporarily the rest of the stage behind them is out of sight of the audience.[42]

---

* Performance cut to 'Do you accept my challenge?'

GIRLS

See! See!

MEN

Make way before us!

GIRLS

Way before them —

MEN

Kneel before us!

GIRLS

Kneel before them —

CHORUS, BOTH MEN AND GIRLS

See! Where
We/They carry on our/their mighty
    shoulder
The Sphinx and the Sibyl rolled in one.
Behold the Oracle![43]

The extempore throne is set down and at the same time Bella pushes her way through the crowd to see what is happening. On recognising the cloaked figure preparing to unmask or lower the bowl from before its face, she runs to it, and Jack, for it is now seen to be he, rises to embrace her.[44]

CHORUS

Jack!
What a trick! What a fraud!
Unscrupulous piece of conjuring!
You're a technician
Not a magician.[45]
Jack of all trades,
What's your role now?
You in that queer cloak and comic hat,
What's your role now?

GIRLS

Dabbling in the magic art!

They all point at Jack.

ALL

The Sorcerer's Apprentice!

They all laugh. A gong sounds. In a single movement the flags and banners [or branches] are lowered and disappear and the Chorus parts in two. In the centre, just below the steps that lead from the upper to the lower stage, therefore almost in a line with the gates and the staircase, is a huge contraption of black veils of roughly human shape, though much more than life-size.

Scene Five. *King Fisher, Bella, Jack, Ancients and Sosostris.*

CHORUS
(*awed at last*)

Sosostris!

Jack places the crystal bowl beside her.

KING FISHER
(*placing himself almost reverentially beside or in front of Sosostris, and speaking almost as if he identified himself with her*)

I needn't tell Madame Sosostris
All the story, for she reads
The past and future like a book.
My only child and daughter Jenifer's
Been kidnapped by these wicked people,*
Locked away behind those gates.
They, past masters of prevarication,
Deny they hold her. But they do.
I failed to make my way by force,
For they can call upon unnatural power.
    (*addressing Sosostris directly*)
Therefore I call on you
To use your visionary powers
To see my daughter where she is,
That I, sustained by your device,
May go to succour her and set her free.
You have no cause to fear their force.
I have no moral need to blench.
A father may protect his child.
Begin the contest!
Examine first the pictures in the bowl
That I may see, find, speak with Jenifer.

He moves aside.

CHORUS

Is there a woman under the black robe?
Will the voice that answers be a god's?

Sosostris's veils begin to wave.

Look! The veils lift on the evening breeze.

SOSOSTRIS
(*in a deep, slow voice*)

Who hopes to conjure with the world of
    dreams,
Waking to life my visionary powers,
He draws inexorably out from the vast
Lottery a dream to dream himself.
The illusion that you practise power is
    delusion.
    (*with gradually rising passion*)
I alone cannot consult myself,
I alone draw out no dream
To dream myself awake.[46]
I dream the shadows that you cast.
I am a medium, not an end.
    (*crying out*)
O my forgotten and forbidden womanhood!

---

* Performance cut to 'for they can call upon unnatural power.'

46

Must I breathe again the perfume that
　　dissolves you?
O bitterness, O bitterness of a Pythia's fate![47]
O body swollen to a monstrous birth!
O horror, horror of transcendent sight![48]
O tongue taught by a god to cry:
'I am what has been, is and shall be,
No mortal ever lifted my garment.'[49]
　　　　　(*calm and with authority*)
You who consult me
Should never doubt me.
Clean let the heart be
Of each seeker.

Truth shall shine through me,　　　　[6]
Once more endue me.
Humble yourselves now,
I speak as a seer.
　　　　　(*in an altered voice*)
Acolyte, acolyte,
Lift up the bowl that I may look.

*Jack holds up the bowl before Sosostris. She
broods over it.*

I see a meadow, fragrant with flowers,
and someone walking there — a girl.

KING FISHER
(*excited*)

Jenifer!

SOSOSTRIS

Fragrant as a flower herself,
She opens her body to the sun.

KING FISHER

My child, alone and safe.

SOSOSTRIS

Oh! But now a lion — [50]
A winged and royal lion —
Enters the flowered field,
Moving with majesty towards the girl.

KING FISHER

Then there's danger.
We must warn her.
This is fearful, to be so near and far.

SOSOSTRIS

The lion has reached the osier bed,
Where she has gone to lie at length.

KING FISHER
(*covering his eyes*)

Oh horrible!

SOSOSTRIS

As the beast rears rampant,
Now I see the face is human
And the wings are arms,
Strong sheltering arms of a manly youth —

KING FISHER

Mark![51]

SOSOSTRIS

The glorious lion of love,
With symbol erect he . . .

KING FISHER
(*rushing forward and forcing Jack to lower
the bowl*)

No! It's all a hoax, a sham,
A cheat fetched out to frighten me.
Your bowl's a useless and disgusting trick.
　　　　　(*snatching the bowl from Jack*)
See, then, what happens to a lie!

*He throws the bowl into the wings, right.
A crash.*

Scene Six. *The same.*

CHORUS
(*sotto voce*)

She saw what happens in the soul.
It's ominous how still she is.

KING FISHER

And now, Sosostris, speak the truth.

CHORUS

Truth is never spoken twice.
It's ominous how still she is.

KING FISHER

Ah! — Does the truth perhaps hurt you?
Are you dumb?

CHORUS

Silence is power.
It's ominous how still she is.

KING FISHER

Jack, take off the robes.
Be quick.
You'll change your part again.

*He gives a sign to Bella, who goes to fetch the
belt and holster from the tree.*

Here, take this belt and holster,
Buckle it fast and so prepare
To do what I command you.

BELLA
(*bringing the belt to Jack*)

O Jack, why did I trust myself and not trust
　　you,
There in the shadow of the wood?

JACK
(*taking off the robes*)

I can't undo this pin here, Bella.
You must help me.

*She does so. The belt is buckled on. They kiss
as though goodbye.*

CHORUS

A brutal dress is a tragic mask
For a fine young man to wear.

Jack comes to King Fisher.

KING FISHER

Since Sosostris will not speak
Then I must speak.
Since Sosostris will not act
Then I must act.
Jack — unveil her.

BELLA
(*crying out*)

Sacrilege! Impious crime!
I hardly know the words I speak,*
But ah, Jack, for our love's sake, now come
away.

KING FISHER
(*shouting*)

This is no time for a whimpering girl.

HE-ANCIENT
(*coming down stage with the She-Ancient to
the edge of the upper stage*)

But time for a man to choose his fate.

CHORUS (MEN)

— for a man to choose his fate.

SHE-ANCIENT

Time for the unborn child to speak.

CHORUS (GIRLS)

— for the unborn child to speak.

BELLA
(*drawing Jack away down stage right*)[52]

Is there not someone waiting to be born,
Some power, some glory, some nativity
Confined to go the way we choose?

JACK

Is there some vision from a world within,
But keener than prudence or precaution,
Revealed to all men if we choose?

CHORUS
(*moving nearer to Jack and Bella and
leaving King Fisher alone, left*)

Dear Jack and Bella, choose for us,
For now we know that we accept
Whatever fate your choice may bring.

THE ANCIENTS
(*moving a little further down stage centre*)

Fate and freedom propound a paradox.
Choose your fate but still the god
Speaks through whatever acts ensue.

KING FISHER
(*going by himself down stage left*)

How am I bounded by their menial choice?
I have provoked it. But not to abdicate
By that one jot or tittle of my power.

*As the ensemble ceases, Bella turns Jack
towards the centre.*

BELLA

Ah, speak, Jack!
Our moment's at its height.

She leads Jack centre to face King Fisher.

JACK

Young though I am,
This is my choice.
I choose to put away disguise.
I choose to strip the veils
Not from Sosostris, but myself.
A builder, I, a builder now,
I choose to throw your badges
At your feet. There!
Take your infernal belt and holster
Back. I care not what you do.
(*turning his back on King Fisher*)
Bella, riding on the great wave's crest, I call.

BELLA

Jack, before it falls like thunder in the
trough, I come.

CHORUS
(*echoing their afternoon song*)

. . . call
Crying as they're flying and this is what
they say:
He must leap and she must fall
When the bright sun shines on midsummer-
day.

Jack and Bella go off right.

KING FISHER
(*shouting after them*)

All right. The wood's watched.
I'll deal with you two later.
Nor can I be baulked by loss of service.

---

* The composer has recommended a cut here, and has supplied a resetting of the text, so that
Bella continues:
But, ah, it's now that a man must choose his fate
(*aside*)
And now that the unborn child shall speak:
(*to Jack*)
Ah, speak, Jack! (*etc.*)

Scene Seven. *The Ancients, King Fisher, Chorus. The Ancients return up stage. King Fisher stoops to pick up the belt and holster, which he buckles on. He turns round to face the Chorus, which is standing between himself and Sosostris. The Chorus draws back reluctantly to give King Fisher access to Sosostris. King Fisher pauses a moment before he lays his hand on the first veil. He begins to unveil her.*

THE ANCIENTS

Pride is virtue in a man of power
If pride is of the virtue not the power.

CHORUS

Look, the sacred veils are flying,
Torn by King Fisher's violent hand.
Black snow flung up against the moon,
Darkening further the darkest hour.[53]

THE ANCIENTS

Pride though where's no reverence
Finds conclusion in catastrophe.[54]

CHORUS

Soon we shall tremble when the heavy
Womb is rent asunder ruthlessly.

At the last veil, King Fisher pauses, for something begins to glow beneath. The glowing increases in intensity.

THE ANCIENTS AND THE CHORUS

Sosostris said:
'I am what has been, is and shall be.
No mortal ever lifted my garment.'

As King Fisher steels himself to seize the last veil, it falls of itself, disclosing an incandescent bud.

CHORUS

Prepare then, all we mortals, then prepare
To turn the face before the face.

The stage is now dark. King Fisher draws back as the bud opens. When the bud is fully open like huge lotus petals on the stage, there is still a gauze over the inner shrine. The Chorus turns away and the gauze falls before the radiant transfiguration,* in reds and gold, of Mark and Jenifer posed in mutual contemplation.† The open petals of the bud form a circle on the ground. Sosostris has vanished.[55]

KING FISHER
(*going down stage*)

Oh, oh — I'm blinded by the sight,
But force myself to look.

CHORUS

Turn the face before the face.

KING FISHER

It's Jenifer, my daughter.
Now Mark, prepare to die.

CHORUS

Turn the face before the face.

KING FISHER
(*taking the pistol from the holster*)

This then is victory.
Jenifer, I free you.

CHORUS

Weep, weep for the impious act.

He aims at Mark. Mark and Jenifer turn their faces towards him in a gesture of power. King Fisher clutches his heart, trembles, and falls to the ground.[57]

Scene Eight. *Ancients, Chorus, later Strephon, Dancers. The men go down stage to King Fisher's body.*

A MAN

King Fisher's dead.

> *The girls recoil together.*

A GIRL

How horrible!

Mark and Jenifer assume a pose of compassion.

HE-ANCIENT
(*coming down the steps on to the lower stage, addressing the men*)

Pride has brought him to the ground.
Carry the King to his grave.

The men lift up the body and slowly carry it up stage and into the temple, whose doors open for them.

MEN
(*repeatedly*)

Lift him now up with our powerful arms,
Letting our tread compose his requiem.

HE-ANCIENT
(*to the girls*)

Gather the veils to make him a shroud.

The girls collect the veils and shroud the body with them.

---

* In Indian mythology, Mark and Jenifer would be transfigured as Shiva-Shakti (Shiva and Parvati). All their gestures and poses are hieratic.
† The outside of Jenifer's right leg is resting on the inside of Mark's left thigh, as they are seated facing the audience, but with their heads turned to each other.[56]

GIRLS
(*repeatedly*)

Mourn not the fall of a man that goes down,
Leaving the room for someone beautiful.

SHE-ANCIENT
(*coming to the footlights and addressing the audience*)

Blessed the dead!
For which of you do minister with love
To the dying under the broken house?
Blessed the dead!

She leaves the centre of the stage.

Strephon comes out of the temple with the dancers, descending on to the lower stage, the men of the Chorus return behind them. The men of the Chorus remain on the upper stage where the girls of the Chorus are already, while Strephon and another dancer come down in front of Mark and Jenifer and begin to make ritual fire. That is, Strephon twirls a pointed stick within a wooden block, which the other dancer holds before him. With the twirling the stick begins to get hot. As the tinder in the block kindles and the stick itself begins to glow, other dancers fan or blow upon the sparks until at last the stick catches fire and after a while Strephon is able to hold the freely burning stick, clear above his head.

The Fourth Dance — Fire in Summer[58]

Mark and Jenifer have relaxed their compassionate pose and assume one of increasing vigour and ecstasy.

CHORUS

Fire! Fire! St John's Fire[59]
In the desert in the night.
Fire! Fire! Fire in summer.

In the first part of the Fire Dance Strephon dances with the lighted stick, while the other dancers force him back towards the transfiguration of Mark and Jenifer until at last he falls at their feet in the pose of a hieratic pedestal. The lighted stick is taken from him and set above and behind the heads of Mark and Jenifer.

MARK AND JENIFER

Sirius rising as the sun's wheel[60]
Rolls over at the utter zenith.
So the dog leaps to the bull[61]
Whose blood and sperm are all fertility.

In the second part of the Fire Dance, the dancers other than Strephon appear by incantatory gestures to cause the lotus petals or other veils to close themselves back over Mark and Jenifer, in such a way that their

bodies disappear from sight from the feet upwards. Strephon is also covered by this means. Finally even the heads disappear and only the lighted stick is visible shining above.

CHORUS
(*on the upper stage, behind the dancers and the transfiguration*)

Carnal love through which the race
Of men is everlastingly renewed
Becomes transfigured as divine
Consuming love whose fires shine
From God's perpetually revealed face.
Wonder! Praise! Rejoice exceedingly!

MARK AND JENIFER

The world is made by our desire,
Its splendour, yes, even its pain
Becomes transfigured in the bright
Furious incandescent light
Of love's perpetually renewed fire.
Wonder! Praise! Rejoice!

THE ANCIENTS
(*down stage*)[62]

From heavenly One the Two divide
And Three as Paraclete can make
Symbolic union with the Four,
The messenger, the path, the door
Between the light and dark, the guide.
Wonder! Praise! Rejoice exceedingly!

When the heads are covered, and the voices have ceased, there is a moment's pause before the lighted stick is drawn down within the veils. The veiled mass glows from within and breaks into flame.

CHORUS

Fire! Fire! St John's Fire.
In the desert in the night.
Fire! Fire! Fire in summer.

Scene Nine. *Finale. Chorus, later Mark, Jenifer. When the flames and ensuing smoke have died down, the stage is very dark, except for moonlight on the white stone of the temple. Strephon, Mark, Jenifer, the Ancients and the Dancers have all vanished.*

CHORUS
(*once more down stage, sotto voce*)*

Even in a summer night
There comes an hour whose cold
Hand fingers the flesh
And chills the hot heart.
For the sun's lost on the night
Journey through the sea and only
Faith that's beyond fear
Trusts tomorrow's morning.[63]

---

* Performance cut, so that the chorus opens with 'Was it a vision?'

The transfiguration at Covent Garden, 1968: Mark (Alberto Remedios) and Jenifer (Joan Carlyle); and 1955 with, from left to right, Edith Coates (She-Ancient), Pirmin Trecu (Strephon), Joan Sutherland (Jenifer), Richard Lewis (Mark) and Michael Langdon (He-Ancient) (photos: Mike Evans, Houston Rogers, Theatre Museum)

O summer sun,
Golden faced
Glorious globe,
Make haste,

Make haste
To find the way
In the dark
To another day.

Was it a vision?
Was it a dream?
In the fading moonlight what shall be seen?

They turn round to look.

Only the temple on the wooded hill,
The gates and the staircase
Cold and still.

But where, where
Are the plighted pair,
The midsummer groom
And bride? Guide
Them safe to our side.

O summer sun,
Golden faced
Glorious globe,
Make haste,

Make haste
To find the way
In the dark
To another day.

The moonlight has faded out and the stage is quite dark. As they remain silent for a while, the birds begin singing before dawn. The stage light returns much as at the beginning of Act One. When it is light enough it will be seen that the temple and the sanctuary of buildings have disappeared once more in the morning mist. The voices of Mark and Jenifer are heard calling off stage. They enter at the same time on opposite sides of the stage, both dressed for their wedding.

MARK

(*coming forward to meet Jenifer with youthful warmth, but dignity*)

Jenifer, Jenifer, my darling . . .
After the visionary night,
The senses purified,
My heart's at rest.

JENIFER

O Mark, truth is assumed
In love so rich.
I could love all —
Even my father had he lived.[64]

MARK

Mourn no stubborn father, but receive the
    ring,
Here in this magic wood on this mid-
    summer day.
'All things fall and are built again
And those that build them again are gay.'[65]

CHORUS

Let us go down the hill with joy
To the bounteous life of this midsummer day.

ALL

'All things fall and are built again
And those that build them again are gay.'[66]

They begin to move off as the sun rises. Their voices disappear in the distance. The stage fills with light. Were the mists to lift again it would be seen that the temple and the sanctuary of buildings were only ruins and stones silhouetted against the clear sky.

Curtain.

'A Visionary Night'
Mark, Act Three

John Lloyd Davies

When *The Midsummer Marriage* was first performed in 1955 critical opinion, while mixed on the merits of the opera as a whole, was united in its hostility to the libretto. Tippett the composer was held to have been let down by Tippett the librettist, and the plot and words were found to be in varying degrees incomprehensible ('meaningless poppycock' as *The People* trenchantly expressed it). Since Tippett is one of the most self-aware and self-analytical creative artists since Wagner, this textual difficulty is not the result of mere operatic incompetence, but rather of an attempt to produce a new kind of operatic work.

Tippett saw, as T. S. Eliot had shown in *The Waste Land*, that modern man languished in a state of spiritual bankruptcy. The scientific and material world had developed to a point where 'technics' overwhelmed the spiritual side of man's nature, and crippled his creative imagination. So Tippett set out to resurrect man's spiritual and imaginative life through an opera which would combine a contemporary social setting with both the ideas of Carl Jung on the development of the personality, and the primitive myths which underlie all human cultures.

Firstly, he wanted his principal couple, Mark and Jenifer, to embody the maturing of the personality which Jung called 'the individuation process'. This is the process by which the personality 'grows up' and comes to terms with its own nature and the world. Thus Mark and Jenifer must learn to understand their subconscious natures, and accept the masculine and feminine parts of their characters. The result is the integration of the psyche in the whole personality, which both characters attain by the end of the opera.

Psychological life does not, however, take place in a vacuum. So Tippett's second theme was growth to social maturity, as exemplified by his second couple, Jack and Bella. During the opera they change from being the unquestioning servants of King Fisher to responsible adults who decide their own future and that of their children.

Tippett's last ingredient for his opera was myth. The main figures and ideas of myth are buried deep in the unconscious of everyone (what Jung called 'the collective unconscious'). Tippett realised that if he could incorporate appropriate mythic material into his story, then the action would be supported by the force of legendary truths (or 'archetypes'). Thus, for example, he derived King Fisher from the Fisher King of the Holy Grail legends. This king suffered from a wound which made him and his lands sterile (comparable to the spiritual sterility of modern society), and only the arrival of a young stranger (i.e. Mark) could lift the curse. Tippett superimposed this myth upon the ancient seasonal rituals known as vegetation rites, in which the annual birth and death of the crops were celebrated at midsummer. In these rites, the old king was ritually killed in order to be replaced by a new king. Tippett's synthesis produced a story in which the exhaustion of modern life, embodied in King Fisher, could only be cured by his death and replacement by Mark. This ritual conclusion reinforces the climax of the psychological development of Mark and Jenifer, and the 'visionary night' ends with Tippett's theme of renewal and rebirth expressed both through the couple's psychological maturity and wholeness, and through the new generation (represented by Mark and Jenifer) taking over from the old (King Fisher). Through the resolution of the conflicts of the opera we experience what Tippett, in his Third Symphony, called 'a huge, compassionate power to heal, to love'.

Tippett's concern in *The Midsummer Marriage* was to 'present a stage of depth', drawing its strength and inspiration from the verse-dramatists of the post-war years. As did Shakespeare in *A Midsummer Night's Dream*, Tippett aimed to 'make play with two worlds of apprehension'. The two worlds — the natural and the supernatural/unconscious — allowed him to present the development and integration of the unconscious in symbolic terms, but without losing sight of the social context within which it is occurring. In 'The Birth of an Opera', Tippett identified four rules which he employed or discovered in relation to the composition of the opera, and which governed its form and content.

The first rule is that 'the verse dramatist carries out on the words themselves artistic operations which the composer effects by music'. As Tippett realised, music provided a unique opportunity to conjure the world of the supernatural, and to solve the verse-dramatist's problem of 'the kind of verse that can sink near to contemporary speech but rise easily to incantation'. The problem for the composer is to create words and music which can embrace both the sublime and the mundane without compromising either. The balance of the two worlds is critical to the success of the opera as a whole, but especially in relation to a character such as King Fisher, who functions simultaneously on a psychological, a social, and several different mythic levels.

Tippett was aiming to create, or effect, a 'collective imaginative experience', but he recognised that 'the great danger is that the symbolical metaphor will be idiosyncratic only, and will never have the power of a collective image'. Thus the creative artist had to be especially sensitive to the power of genuine archetypes, and not manufacture arbitrary symbols of his own. Tippett's second rule is that 'the more collective an artistic imaginative experience is going to be, the more the discovery of suitable material is involuntary.' This explains the lengthy gestation period of the opera, while Tippett searched literary, mythological and anthropological texts for the material which would exactly express his intention. His first inspiration, that of the wooded hill-top with the characters of his principal couple, fulfilled this requirement: involuntary inspiration had put him in touch with a powerful archetype of the collective unconscious. Tippett knew that he was on the right track: he experienced 'the feeling a creative artist has when he knows he has become the instrument of some collective imaginative experience — or, as Wagner put it, that a Myth is coming once more to life'.

But the use of mythic material is not confined merely to repeating the legends and archetypes of the past. The corollary is Tippett's third rule: 'while the collective mythological material is always traditional, the specific twentieth century quality is the power to transmute such material into an immediate experience of our day.' Thus the success or failure of the use of mythic material in the opera will depend on Tippett's ability to re-cast the myths in a form which is simultaneously eternal and contemporary. Again, the music enables this fusion to take place, as stated in Tippett's fourth rule 'that in opera the musical schemes are always dictated by the situations'. The delicate transition between the banal and the ineffable must be effected musically and convince the audience that the two interwoven worlds form a coherent fabric.

The Midsummer Marriage is concerned with renewal, and a renewal in which the audience can participate. In line with the Jungian view that dreams are an attempt by the unconscious mind to sort and solve problems of the individual personality, the opera can be seen as a dream, 'drawn inexorably out from the vast lottery', in which the audience can resolve and heal itself. If criteria of causal logic and motivation are applied to the opera, it does indeed appear confused. It is necessary to surrender to the work as to a dream, and allow it to establish its own logic and mythic necessity. As Tippett says, only if the music can invoke the supernatural world and 'suspend the critical and analytical judgement' can the work communicate its true meanings.

Notes on the text of 'The Midsummer Marriage'

1 Strephon plays a flute — the instrument commonly used at vegetation rites, owing to its suggestion of sexual fertility (*cf* Pan). The flute also possesses qualities of spirituality and power, as seen in its use and significance in Mozart's *The Magic Flute*.
2 Mark *runs* on — at his first appearance we see him as the embodiment of life and vitality. His strength at the opening of the opera contrasts with the entry of Tamino in *The Magic Flute*, who is exhausted and immediately faints. Mark breaks up the dance, the first indication of the disruptive influence of new life. As yet he is not spiritually mature, therefore (as in the similar scene in Bernard Shaw's *Back to Methuselah*), he does not value the spiritual life of the Ancients.
3 'Strange was my birth' — in the Grail legends and vegetation rites, it must be a stranger, or holy fool, who replaces the old king and lifts the curse of sterility (*cf Parsifal*).
4 Strephon's injury prefigures the wounds of the Ritual Dances. Progress and transformation involve pain (*cf* initiation rites). The extreme example of this is that for Mark and Jenifer, the final stage in the individuation process can only be achieved at the cost of King Fisher's death. The tripping of Strephon is a concrete example of traditional beauty (the dance) destroyed.
5 *The Chorus returns* — they have been *witnesses* in the sacred wood, watching the enactment of the ritual, just as the audience witnesses the enactment of the opera.
6 Mark's aria is joyous and celebratory, an example of the romanticism in English art which blossomed immediately after the Second World War. Similar sentiments may be found in the work of Christopher Fry and Dylan Thomas, which abounds with vitality and the spirit of regeneration. Mark's Dionysiac energy contrasts with Tamino's more reflective Portrait Aria: in Tippett's opera, his hero and heroine represent opposing tendencies (mind and body) which must be reconciled.
7 Jenifer seeks to go beyond the temporal world, into a contemplative retreat. *cf* T.S. Eliot's *Ash Wednesday*:
> The Lady is withdrawn
> In a white gown, to contemplation, in a white gown.
8 'Don't touch me' — *cf Methuselah*, Chloe: 'Don't! We can talk quite well without touching each other.' Mark's attempts to win Jenifer have extended to the physical, which she resists because of her pursuit of spiritual enlightenment. He cannot understand her reaction because of his own Dionysiac tendency.
9 The voice of Sosostris warns King Fisher — the oracle prophesies the danger of his pursuit. As in all mythology, however, the forbidden act is the act which must be committed. In Eden it was necessary for the apple to be eaten for the myth to

function. Prophetic warnings are always ignored, disbelieved or misconstrued: *cf* the Delphic oracle, and Cassandra. King Fisher's fate also has the inevitability of myth. (See note 41 below).

10 Transfigurations — Athene, the female equivalent of Apollo, is the opposite of Dionysus. She represents purity and wisdom. She can also be the goddess of the hunt (*cf* the female role as pursuer in the Ritual Dances). Zeus learned that the children of his first wife Metis would live to depose him, so he ate her. He was then struck by a headache, which Hephaestus cured by splitting his head open with an axe, whereupon Athene appeared, fully-grown from his skull. Thus Athene comes from Zeus's head (mind), whilst Dionysus (son of Semele) had a second birth from Zeus's thigh. The duality of mind and body is thus evident even in their origins. Dionysus (Bacchus) is the god of wine, flesh and fertility, and is frequently a central figure in vegetation rites. The divine union of Athene and Dionysus is analogous to that of Isis and Osiris, the parallel Egyptian deities (*cf The Magic Flute*).

11 *cf The Odyssey*, 'a wine-dark sea'. Red is the colour of vitality and passion, while white is the colour of serenity and spiritual purity. The 'swan-white sky' suggests the rape of Leda by Jupiter as a swan (*cf* Yeats's poem *Leda and the Swan*).

12 'I am a child of starry heaven . . . of the fruitful earth' — these lines are taken from the epigraph to the opera which comes from the Petelia Tablet, one of the Orphic tablets of the 4th century BC, found in graves in Crete and Southern Italy. The text was intended to be worn as an amulet when passing through the underworld. As Kemp (*see Bibliography*) shows, it is significant in several respects. The opera itself represents an amulet for the journey the audience is about to engage upon, through an initiation of psychological and mythic development. But the epigraph also expresses the Jungian duality evident throughout the opera: after their first journeys, Mark is a child of earth (Dionysus) and Jenifer a child of heaven (Athene). They must fulfil their development in order to become children of both earth *and* heaven. Thus the motto is both a Jungian and a mythic commentary on the opera.

13 'what outer darkness' — Mark is drawn towards the anima by his own psyche.

14 'a deeper dark' — *ie* the unconscious.

15 'gate of horn' — the gate to the underworld through which dreams were supposed to pass on their way to the world of man: *cf Aeneid* VI 892ff and *Odyssey* XIX 559ff. The name also refers to the central altar at Stonehenge, which gave access to the supernatural world.

16 Mark goes downwards into the unconscious, into the anima to confront his own dark side. This idea may also be seen in the myths of Orpheus, Osiris and Christ, who each descend temporarily into the underworld in order to rise again. Dante uses the same theme in his progression through *Inferno* and *Purgatorio* to *Paradiso*, as does Eliot in *Burnt Norton*, III:

Descend lower, descend only,
Into the world of perpetual solitude.

Tippett himself had employed the idea of a descent into the unconscious in *A Child of Our Time*:

The world descends into the icy waters,
Where lies the jewel of great price.

17 'a boat across the water' — a sea journey is often used in myth as a symbol for the voyage into the unconscious. *cf* Charon's boat across the Styx to Hades (*The Waste Land*), and Dante crossing Acheron, the river of death. The connection is the significance of water, symbolising the unconscious, the journey through the underworld (Eliot: 'In a drifting boat with a slow leakage', *The Dry Salvages*, II). But its significance is also related to the vegetation rites: the sun, when it sets, is supposed to undergo a night journey under the Western ocean to reappear in the East next day. (See also note 39 below.)

18 The silver trumpet sounded behind Jenifer and the cymbals sounded behind Mark symbolise the nature of the first part of their quest. The silver trumpet makes a pure, spiritual sound, whereas the cymbals make a rhythmic, vital clash of Dionysiac passion. In his evocation of the 'stallions stamping' Tippett again sounds the note of post-war romanticism (*cf* Dylan Thomas's 'The force that through the

green fuse'), and also reveals his kinship with the verse of Walt Whitman.

19 The central inquiry in J.G. Frazer's *The Golden Bough* is into the meaning of the ritual of the Golden Bough in the sacred wood at Nemi. In this ritual a bough had to be torn from the sacred oak tree by the new king, and used as a weapon to slay the old king. (See note 23 below.)

20 A reference to sacrificial rites — in *Moving Into Aquarius* Tippett quotes accounts of concentration camp ramps where children were trodden to death in the panic. Tippett is indicating that Dionysiac passion has a darker side.

21 *ie* Life in the context of death, passion arising from mortality. Here the duality is of love and death, Eros and Thanatos (postulated by Freud as the two great instincts of human life). Life involves and implies death. Mark's life means King Fisher's death.

22 By the use of the mirror, Jenifer attempts to show Mark his darker side, revealing the unconscious (as, in myth, a mirror is used to see Medusa, the Gorgon, a symbol of the dark side of the psyche). According to Frazer, many primitives believe photographs or images of themselves in a mirror to be their real (unconscious) souls. Jenifer shows Mark the dangers of instinct without a controlling consciousness.

23 'golden branch' — a reference to the Golden Bough. According to the rite of the sacred wood at Nemi (see note 19 above), the branch was the symbol and weapon of the new king. It is also, according to Greek mythology, the symbol of Dionysus's power (a golden wand), a symbol of virility and living strength.

24 'serpent' — image of negative power.
'saint' — idealised Jenifer. She realises that such a dichotomy cannot reconcile the lovers, so she goes to confront her own shadow side.
'go to find the beast' — (in original manuscript — 'slay') — a common myth is that of St George (the young hero) slaying the dragon (Dionysiac lust) and saving the maiden (purity). Tippett changed his text because this idea is one of light triumphing over dark, not a Jungian reconciliation of both sides of the personality.

25 Reference to St Joan — Tippett borrowed this from F. Wimwar's biography (letter to E. Walter White, September 14, 1949). Joan heard inspirational voices, which were an experience of the eternal, at high noon (*cf* midsummer), and was filled with *animus* (the male strength and will to fight).
'the summer sun' — the flame of sunlight prefigured the flames in which she would be martyred. This incident also prefigures the lotus and the Fire Dance of Act Three.

26 Path from heaven to hell (see note 62 below) — road to enlightenment; as with Dante and Blake, the road to spiritual maturity involves going through innocence and experience to a restored innocence, which is founded in experience. Jung saw this reconciled synthesis as the resolution of the dualities of the personality.

27 Mark and Jenifer are the royal couple. They are both representatives of the Chorus, and they are also a point of contact with the eternal. In the vegetation rites, the king was seen as a man-god who acted as intercessor between his people and the gods. The Chorus call themselves 'laughing children' (*cf* Eliot, *Burnt Norton*, III:
The leaves were full of children,
Hidden excitedly, containing laughter)
and they need Mark and Jenifer as an example for their own growth.

28 'She must leap and he must fall' — an example of Jungian duality. To achieve wholeness it is necessary for Mark and Jenifer to go both up and down. *cf* epigraph to *The Four Quartets*, 'The road up and down is the same road' — Heraclitos.

29 Jack's passivity here is in contrast with his assertiveness after the third Ritual Dance. The Ritual Dances have an effect on him, too, though not one of transcendence: like Raskolnikov in *Crime and Punishment*, who dreams of a passive horse, beaten to death, and thus determines to *act*, Jack sees the ritual destruction of Strephon as an indicator that he should fight back against King Fisher and be positive and decisive.

30 *cf The Magic Flute* — Papageno/Papagena duet. The similarities are very close, both couples concentrating on domestic bliss, and seeing the central facts of their marriage as home and children, rather than seeking a spiritual and bodily relationship for its own sake (*cf* Mark and Jenifer in Act Three).

31 *The trees appear to move* — the dancers can be seen as tree-spirits. In vegetation rites, the trees of the sacred wood contain the spirits of gods or the ancestral fathers. In this form of animism, the wood becomes the repository of all past tradition.

32 The origin of the themes of the Ritual Dances lies in Robert Graves's *The White Goddess*, which concerns a Welsh myth of the cyclic life and death (and subsequent resurrection) of the God of the Waxing Year. In this legend, the God fights unsuccessfully against the God of the Waning Year (the God's own shadow) for the love of the White Goddess. The relevance of this myth to the stories of the vegetation rites is clear. Graves includes an account of the *Romance of Taliesin*, in which a young warrior Gwion (the youthful stranger) accidentally tasted a drop from a brew prepared by the goddess Cerridwen and received enlightenment (*cf* Siegfried and Fafner's blood in *The Ring* cycle). Cerridwen pursued Gwion (male pursued by female). He turned himself into a hare, she turned into a hound; he turned into a fish, she became an otter; he turned into a bird, she became a hawk. Then he turned himself into a grain of wheat, and she became a chicken and ate him. Cerridwen became pregnant and gave birth to Gwion. Thus we see the idea of the adoption of animal guises as an integral part of the mythological treatment of sexual relations; Tippett's use of this mythic material is fully examined in Kemp (*op.cit.*).

Tippett uses the first three pursuits in their original form, but adapts the last so that Mark and Jenifer are reborn out of the shell of Sosostris together. In the first three dances, Strephon, the male *animus* figure of the mind, is pursued by a girl dancer who embodies the female *anima* qualities of instinct. The point of the dances is to show the logical male world of the mind being caught up and assimilated by the instinctive world of the subconscious emotions. It is not clear why Tippett did not name his other dancer — some commentators suggest that he intends the opera to stress only Mark's development. But this conclusion seems unjustified given the exact and intimate equality of Mark and Jenifer in Act Three, and Tippett's own explanation of the dances: 'Mark and Jenifer go through a series of ritual trials that are symbolically realised in ballet, the first three Ritual Dances.' The dances clearly apply to both Mark and Jenifer, since the male being caught by the female is also the mind being caught by the body: the resolution of both dualities is necessary for wholeness.

The other important aspect of the Ritual Dances is Tippett's use of the four elements and the four seasons. His association of these with his four dances is significant in several respects: firstly it binds the heart of the work firmly to the seasonal cycle, reinforcing the theme of renewal already implicit in the vegetation rites. Secondly, the use of the elements provides a fundamental link with the raw matter of creation (*cf* Shiva dancing the world into existence). Thirdly, the order of the elements, which fits the procession of the seasons, also conveys the development of mankind. In a letter of September 14, 1949, Tippett writes of having discovered a parallel use of the elements in Yeats:

> He with body waged a fight;
> Body won and walks upright. (Earth)
> Then he struggled with the heart;
> Innocence and peace depart. (Water)
> Then he struggled with the mind;
> His proud heart he left behind. (Air)
> Now his wars with God begin;
> At stroke of midnight God shall win. (Fire)

This process of physical and psychological development is strikingly similar to Tippett's treatment in the opera, ending in a final religious transcendence through fire. It is also worth noting that the terrain of the dances becomes increasingly liquid and free: earth, water, air, fire.

The increasing severity of the wounds received by Strephon are the necessary pain involved in any process of transformation or initiation rite. The wound which Strephon received when he was tripped in Act One (showing the pain that change will cost Mark), is a pre-echo of this systematic wounding. The climax of the pursuits is death, that creative death which leads to rebirth and renewal, but Jack and Bella cannot directly understand this, which is why Bella is disturbed by the ritual. The final completion of the ritual development in fact depends on another death — that of King Fisher — after which the fourth dance can take place.

33 'Take me away, I can't bear it' — Bella cannot bear exposure to the rigours of the supernatural world (cf Papageno's reactions to the trials in *The Magic Flute*). As Eliot says: 'Human kind cannot bear very much reality.' *Burnt Norton*, I.

34 'the real Bella' — yes, but is it? She puts on a mask (persona) to approach the world. Tippett does not explore this aspect.

35 'O-hay, O-hay' — this melisma is common in Cornish folksong. Tippett was especially interested in the ecstatic melismas found in glossolalia — religiously inspired 'speaking in tongues'. He uses it here as a wordless expression of joy. (cf Wagner, who frequently used wordless melismatic cries for heightened vocal effect, eg Senta's ballad in *The Flying Dutchman*, Brünnhilde's war-cry in *The Valkyrie* etc.)

36 The normal practice at vegetation rites was to have a ceremonial feast before the ritual sacrifice. Thus Tippett introduces a celebratory meal before the climactic events of the opera. Bread and wine were universally used; the wine as a symbol of Dionysus, the bread as an invocation of the corn-god. Fishes were eaten in ceremonies pertaining to the Fisher King. The obvious parallel is the Christian Last Supper and Eucharist: the bread and wine commemorating Christ's body and blood, and the fish being an early Christian symbol.

37 'man is a god, so he thinks' — this is Dionysiac delusion: there is only flesh and vitality here. Sosostris needs to contribute spiritual wisdom before integration can be achieved.

38 The Half-Tipsy Man fulfils the same role as Jack impersonating Sosostris: he is the Jungian 'Trickster' — the cunning or comic figure, whose irreverence towards the real power of the myth throws the genuine ritual into greater relief. The Half-Tipsy Man's interruption of the dance echoes the serious tripping of Strephon in Act One. There is also the point that Dionysus, despite vitality, is too drunk and clumsy to dance: dancers must have life *and* control, and are thus a counterpart in movement to the spiritual development of Mark and Jenifer. (cf epigraph to *The Waste Land*, where Trimalchio challenges the Sybil, who, like Sosostris, is burdened by her gift.)

39 The sun's journey after setting in the Western ocean in order to rise again in the East. This was conceived as being analogous to the soul's journey through the underworld. It is of particular significance that the moon is at the full, since in many primitive societies the king is replaced or challenged every eight years because only then is the lunar calendar in exact synchronisation with the solar calendar at midsummer: *ie* there is a full moon at the summer solstice. Such a time is even more especially a time of transformation and strangeness. The moon is referred to as 'the white goddess' (see note 32 above), who symbolises purity and serenity, and is identified with Athene/Isis/Shakti. The moon's 'airborne journey' is the counterpart of the sun's undersea journey. The sun/moon polarity echoes the summer/winter one: the summer solstice, the high point of summer, is also the point at which winter begins.

40 The holster hung on the tree echoes other mythic instances of weapons coming from trees — Wotan's spear, Siegmund's sword. It also hints at the Golden Bough itself, which came from the sacred oak.

41 The He-Ancient's warning is a ritual warning, not a real attempt to prevent King Fisher. The myth *requires* the performance of the forbidden action (see note 9).

42 Procession: cf procession with egg in *Back to Methuselah*. Kemp (*op. cit.*) suggests a parallel with the ritual of Jack-in-the-Green, where the ailing god was carried, wearing a conical hat and cloak, and then ritually burnt. This is paralleled in the final burning of the lotus.

43 'oracle' — Tippett based Sosostris's aria on the poem *La Pythie* by Valéry about the burdens of the Pythia, who was the voice of the Delphic oracle. This oracle was noted for its ambiguous prophecies: eg it told Croesus that if he crossed the River Halys to fight a battle he would destroy a great kingdom — Croesus crossed the river, only to discover that the kingdom referred to was his own.

44 Jack functions as a version of the Trickster myth — the false hero, whose appearance highlights the eventual genuine one. This incident also shows, however, that none of the Chorus can tell a real supernatural being from a false one.

45 'a technician, not a magician' — Tippett's point is that technical skills cannot fulfil the functions of the real imagination and the real supernatural.

46 While the creative artist can affect the lives of other people, his own life is always lived at one remove from reality. This self-consciousness prevents the artist from being free to be completely spontaneous as a human being. Thus the artist is condemned by his creative ability to a life which can only consist of realising his art. In Sosostris, Tippett is presenting the dilemma of the artist, cursed and blessed by a gift which can only bring succour to others, not to himself.

47 Myth of the Pythia: fated to lose her womanhood and yet to give painful birth to the inspiration of Apollo. (Since Apollo is identified with Athene, the wisdom connection leads back to Jenifer in Act One; Sosostris is the counter-active spiritual force to the Dionysiac tendency in the Chorus at the start of this act.)

48 'The horror, the horror' — Kurtz's final words in Conrad's novel *Heart of Darkness*. He has seen into the heart of darkness, *ie* the utter bottom of man's Dionysiac tendencies, and the horror has killed him. Eliot's work includes several references to Conrad, and the idea behind Kurtz's death is similar to Eliot's assertion that 'human kind cannot bear very much reality'. King Fisher dies because he cannot bear the spiritual reality which is revealed to him. *cf* the Ancient in *Back to Methuselah*; 'one moment of the ecstasy of life as we live it would strike you dead.'

49 This couplet, taken from a Schiller poem, was kept by Beethoven on his desk. The first line also has biblical precedents: God says to the Israelites 'I am what I am'. It is the idea of the eternal, unchanging oracle.
'lifted my garment' — although Sosostris is destined to dispense timeless inspiration, no-one will discover the source of her wisdom. It is an open question whether Tippett meant the appearance of Mark and Jenifer from the shell of Sosostris to signify that inspiration comes from an integrated personality and sexual/psychological union; or whether inspiration is an eternal mystery, and the couple emerge from Sosostris because, on this occasion, *they* are her prophecy to King Fisher. The latter seems more likely.

50 'Winged and royal lion' — the Christian emblem for St Mark. The lion symbolises masculinity and kingship.

51 It is arguable that only shame at the recognition of his own represented incestuous desires is sufficient motive for King Fisher to die — in this way his death is almost a self-willed suicide.

52 Bella is concerned about her responsibility to her future children. Jack is dimly aware of the other world, which inspires him with a thought 'keener than prudence' to reject King Fisher. Moral choice is 'revealed to all men if we choose'.
The Ancients' paradox — *cf* Jung's inscription over his front door, from the Delphic oracle, 'Invoked or not invoked, the god is present'. The paradox of the relationship between fate and freedom was to form the central question of *King Priam*.

53 This section functions as a 'parabasis' — a Greek choric commentary sung directly to the audience. The Ancients state that virtue should be pursued for its own sake, not for the power it may bring, while the Chorus recoil from the sacrilege of King Fisher unveiling Sosostris, describing it as 'black snow against the moon' *ie* impurity against the pure White Goddess. For the first time in the opera, King Fisher is taking personal action (not commanding others), venting his anger on the veils.

54 'catastrophe' — the fall resulting from King Fisher's hubris.
'womb is rent asunder' — the womb of Sosostris as the Earth-mother (*cf* Erda) produces Mark and Jenifer (*cf* Brünnhilde).

55 Lotus bud — Hindu symbol of wholeness, *cf* Eliot, *The Four Quartets*:
The lotus rose, quietly, quietly . . .

56 *Mark and Jenifer are in a pose of perpetual contemplation* — the pose which Tippett so exactly describes comes from Hindu sacred art (Kemp, pages 491/2 *op. cit*), and the royal couple, representing psychic totality described by Zimmer in *Myths and Symbols in Indian Art* are 'imbued with the secret knowledge that, though

seemingly two, they are fundamentally one. For the sake of the universe and its creatures, the Absolute (represented by the lotus) has apparently unfolded into this duality, and out of them derive all the life polarities.' Shiva, simultaneously the Destroyer and the god who danced the universe into existence, and Shakti, his bride, the Earth Mother. This conjunction of opposites is only possible at the turning point of midsummer. As Eliot says of incarnation:

> Here the impossible union
> Of spheres of existence is actual,
> Here the past and future
> Are conquered, and reconciled.

57   King Fisher's death is not willed by Mark and Jenifer. Rather, when they turn to face him, he receives the full force of the revelation, which kills him. *cf* Part IV of *Methuselah*, the Elderly Gentleman dies because transcendence is too much for him. As we have seen, King Fisher's death is mythologically and psychologically necessary for the new life of Mark and Jenifer. His death is not that of a hated villain, but that of a necessary player in a mythic ritual, *cf* Eliot, *Burnt Norton*, V:

> That which is living
> Can only die.

Thus his death is neither rejoiced nor mourned, except in ritual terms.

58   The Fourth Ritual Dance: Fire in Summer — During the course of the dance, the bud containing Mark and Jenifer closes around them, engulfing them in flame, which symbolises both their completion of the psychological 'individuation process' and their mythic transcendence. For they have arrived at the condition of 'self', complete wholeness and self-integration. Much of the thinking behind Tippett's use of the Fire-dance is derived from Eliot's *Four Quartets*, especially the last quartet, *Little Gidding*. In this, Eliot uses the dual image of fire, and the symbol of the lotus, to express the way in which transcendence is possible:

> From wrong to wrong the exasperated spirit
> Proceeds, unless restored by that refining fire
> Where you must move in measure, like a dancer.

Tippett takes up this idea to express the fire of transcendence through dance. Eliot's final lines of reconciliation and transcendence are, likewise, the key to Tippett's whole intention in the opera:

> A condition of complete simplicity
> (Costing not less than everything)
> And all shall be well and
> All manner of thing shall be well
> When the tongues of flame are in-folded
> Into the crowned knot of fire
> And the fire and the rose are one.

In the Fire-dance, Mark and Jenifer are totally consumed, and Strephon (Mark's shadow) is finally absorbed into Mark's personality, and disappears in the flames. Mark and Jenifer's absorption in flame also corresponds to the voluntary human sacrifice, practised in some cultures, where the old king (or a representative of him) would be thrown into the flames of the midsummer fire for the new king to rise again. Mark and Jenifer's duet employs such extensions of vowel sound that the words become virtual melismas of sound, the expression, as we have seen, of transcendent ecstasy. Their duet, unlike that in Act One, is completely reconciled and harmonious. Tippett's use of Hindu deities for this scene is partly the result of the lack of a suitable image from Christianity, and partly from a wish not to use explicitly Christian material, because it is so compromised for a modern audience, for whom established Christianity is a staid and rather conventional institution. The Church's horror of sexuality means that Tippett had no Christian image of sexual unity on which to draw, and his invocation of Hinduism parallels Eliot's use of Sanskrit at the end of *The Waste Land*: 'Shantih, Shantih, Shantih', the Sanskrit equivalent of 'the peace which passeth all understanding'. Eliot chose the former not just because it widened the scope of the poem, but also because he felt the Christian phrase to be 'worked out' by meaningless repetition, and to have lost all its original force as a prayer. Ananda Coomoaraswamy observed in 1921 the 'cult' of oriental imitation in Western art, and commented 'The chaotic character of modern Western art is the symptom of its lack of inner necessity . . . an ancient art may be a source of inspiration.' In using an Eastern image for his scene of reconciliation and resolution, Tippett is trying to re-introduce that 'inner necessity' into fragmented Western art.

59 'Fire!' — *cf* midsummer fire-festivals, linked with vegetation rites. 'St John's fire, in the desert' refers to the fact that the Christian Church took over the primitive festivals by making them refer to John the Baptist. Mark and Jenifer's pose of 'increasing vigour and ecstasy' is clearly meant to be ritual copulation. Fire in these festivals has two significances: it is a symbolic fire of purification (*Golden Bough*, X; also Eliot, *Little Gidding*:

> The only hope, or else despair,
> Lies in the choice of pyre or pyre —
> To be redeemed from fire by fire.)

But the fire also symbolises 'the compelling fire which can consummate a transforming union of opposites'. In both mythology and alchemy it is fire which can synthesize opposing forces and materials in a whole and complete union.

60 'Sirius rising' — *Golden Bough*: 'In the early days of Egyptian history, the splendid star of Sirius . . . appeared at dawn in the East at the summer solstice, and marked the beginning of the sacred year.'

61 'the dog leaps to the bull' — Sirius (the Dog Star) rises into Taurus at midsummer, the bull motif continuing since the bull represents Dionysus and fertility. Thus Sirius, the star of spirit, Isis/Athene, meets with Taurus, the sign of Dionysus and fertility. The bull was sacrificed at Mithraic and Dionysiac vegetation rites, and its blood drunk, after which there was reconciliation and peace and the land was fertile.

62 Ancients:

One = original creation, God, ground of all being.

Two = creation divided into dualities, light/dark, male/female, *cf* 'The Tao, the undivided, Great One, gives rise to two opposite reality principles, the dark and the light, Yin and Yang.' (*The Secret of the Golden Flower*, ed. Wilhelm and Jung).

Three =(a) male principle, *animus*, mind.

   (b) Paraclete, *ie* Holy Spirit, third part of the Trinity.

Four = (a) female principle, *anima*, body.

   (b) divine wholeness and integrity, the seasons, the elements.

   (c) four parts of Jungian individuation process (shadow, *animus/a*, *mana* personality, self).

Union of Three and Four = Seven, divine creativity. Tippett appears to suggest that the Christian Trinity *can* be reconciled with the Jungian four ways and primitive seasonal rites.

Chorus:

'Carnal love, through which the race / Of men is everlastingly renewed, / Becomes transfigured as divine / Consuming love whose fires shine / From God's perpetually revealed face.' *ie* the purely biological sexual function can be transfigured as the summit of psychological and supernatural reconciliation and maturity.

63 'only faith that's beyond fear trusts to tomorrow's morning' — necessity of faith in cycle of existence, *cf* Blake,

> If the Sun or Moon should doubt
> They'd immediately
> Go out.

64 'even my father' — King Fisher seen as necessary part of ritual, not as evil villain.

65 'All things fall and are built again, / And those that build them again are gay.' From W. B. Yeats's poem *Lapis Lazuli*, celebrating the cyclic nature of all life, the creative joy of new life.

66 'let us go down the hill' — back into normal life, integrated and reconciled by the spiritual events of the visionary night.

Pirmin Trecu as Strephon in the world première at Covent Garden in 1955, choreography by John Cranko (photo: Houston Rogers, Theatre Museum)

Mark (John Treleaven) and Jenifer (Felicity Lott) are finally united, Welsh National Opera, 1977 (photo: Julian Sheppard)

Howard Haskin as Paris in the Kent Opera production, 1984 (photo: Roger de Wolf)

Music for an Epic

Andrew Clements

Tippett began work on *King Priam* in 1958, some six years after completing *The Midsummer Marriage*. The impulses which led him to the choice of a classical subject for his second opera were characteristically various. The visits to London in 1956 of Brecht's Berliner Ensemble and Jean-Louis Barrault's company alerted the composer to the possibility of utilising the approach of the epic theatre, presenting a story in a series of scenes and commentaries absolutely on its own terms, extracting its essence without any kind of adulteration. In his mind grew a vague plan for a dramatic work of eight loosely connected scenes, a scenario which at that stage might as easily have produced a cantata or ballet as an opera. After further refinement and taking advice, however, Tippett settled on an opera, but from the outset determined that it would be far removed from *The Midsummer Marriage* in dramatic treatment and subject matter; this would be a tragedy, and one derived from classical legend, in this case the story of King Priam and the fall of Troy.

Choice of subject determined the musical language; there would be no question here of the essentially lyrical impulse which had fashioned its predecessor. Tippett's concert works from the years after *The Midsummer Marriage* inhabit the same enchanted sound-world of efflorescent lines and richly coloured harmonies; only in the Second Symphony of 1957 is there a hint of the harder edges and more abrasive textures that might be appropriate for a drama in which what the composer called 'the mysterious nature of human choice' and its futility when confounded by fate would be the central theme. Yet the language which Tippett developed for *King Priam* represented a far more radical departure from his previous music than even the Second Symphony might have suggested. What was required was a highly flexible, absolutely direct style, lean and bright-textured. Classical concepts of thematic development would be out of place in a scheme which presented the action in sharply characterised scenes, with the minimum of preparation and very little attempt to give the protagonists an existence beyond their relevance to the plot. Hearing Stravinsky's ballet *Agon* in 1957 gave Tippett the clue he needed: spareness would be the key to *Priam*, characters would be accompanied by a minimum of instruments, often just a solo line. Development would be replaced by repetition and superimposition; elaborate tonal plans become irrelevant when the musical language itself sometimes maintains only the most tenuous links with tonality, and give way to a mosaic construction composed of self-contained paragraphs.

It is remarkable that within a single work Tippett should have evolved this startlingly different idiom and deployed it to such brilliant effect. For the matching of character, theme and instrumental colour is most cunningly done, allowing the composer to set up highly subtle musical relationships between individuals in different sections of the opera. So though the opera opens with raw trumpet calls and the offstage shouts of the chorus conjuring up 'the plains of windy Troy', we already hear in this short prelude the seeds of destruction; the chorus's cries herald the birth of Paris, fated to cause the death of his father Priam and the downfall of Troy, and the same music will recur in modified form when the city burns in the final scene. Paris's instrument, it soon becomes obvious, is the oboe; a simple dotted theme introduces him as a baby in a cradle, and as he grows to manhood through the act his music will become ever more elaborate and sophisticated. His nurse rocks the cradle to an accompanying harp figure which will return later in the scene when Priam remembers that he was once a baby also.

Hecuba, wife of Priam, mother of Paris, has had a nightmare; her agitated theme is heard in a preliminary form at this point on the piano, which throughout the opera functions as a kind of neutral, non-aligned accompanist. Not until Priam's arrival do we get the first full-blooded thematic statement. His is a theme of undoubted regal bearing, but at the same time it contains its own contradictions, as piano octaves and horn move in clashing contrary motion:

[1] PRIAM

The Old Man called to interpret Hecuba's dream brings his own instrumental retinue of bass clarinet, bassoon and double bassoon that will characterise each of his appearances. His interpretation — that the infant will cause its father's death — brings the first appearance of the 'death' motif, whose shrill sound-world of high woodwind and pitched percussion is later to be closely identified with the messenger Hermes, ironic agent of death and destruction:

[2]

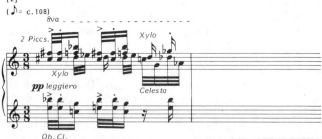

Hecuba's reaction, 'Then I am no longer mother to this child', triggers off the agitated, neo-classical violin figuration which defines her character for the rest of the opera, and for the first time introduces a key signature and a definite key, D major:

[3]

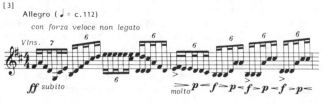

She has no doubts of her duty to her husband and to Troy; hence, perhaps, the tonal certainty of her music. But when Priam begins to deliver his decision he cannot summon the same conviction, despite the relative richness of his string accompaniment:

[4] PRIAM

Andante (♪ = c. 96)

This is the first of the substantial monologues which Tippett gives to Priam, and which chart the progressive hopelessness of his position, as he sees his freedom of choice inexorably negated by fate. These arias of decision serve both a dramatic and a musical function, not only keeping the audience aware of the psychological condition of the opera's central character — it is after all called *King Priam* and not *Helen and Paris* — but providing points of repose and reflection for the listener, a relief from the declamation and hard instrumental edges that move the action forward, and a palpable, if invariably transient, excursion into expressive territory that is more inward and smoothly contoured.

Scenes one and two are separated by the first interlude, in which a Chorus of three — the Old Man, the Nurse, and the Young Guard who was dispatched to kill Paris — break out of their roles to address the audience directly. The interludes serve as both commentary and narration, moving the action forward in the most economical way while at the same time crystallising the dilemmas facing the principal characters, and reminding us once more that this is to be Priam's tragedy, and that his dilemma lies at the heart of the opera. The Chorus's vocal trio develops over clipped, martial chords and running neo-baroque figuration; it leads directly into the second scene, which takes place a decade or so later, with Troy 'calm and flourishing; occasion for hunting and the arts of peace'.

Priam and his elder son Hector are out hunting; the horns initiate a bucolic 'hunting' scherzo whose motifs alternate with a rising and falling major third on the flute and piccolo which seems to evoke again the rawness of the Trojan countryside. This angular, rather schematic writing is arrested by one of the score's most telling moments — Paris appears as a boy and his innocent treble voice is heralded by music of enormous sophistication and sensuousness, a sudden magical return to the enchantment of *The Midsummer Marriage* as the strings divide into finely-spun sustained chords, decorated by the harp. The solo oboe soon insinuates itself into this texture, and goes on to underpin the discussion between Priam and Hector over the boy's future; it withdraws only when Priam begins the second of his monologues, in which he accepts the decision of fate to return his second son to him, finally summoning the characters who make up the Chorus to witness his decision. The second interlude, 'Life is a bitter charade', veers between langourous, unaccompanied melismata and dry, cynical observation until it merges into the celebrations for the wedding of Hector and Andromache. The description of the ceremony as it emerges in conversational fragments is accompanied by running figuration shared between the piano and strings. After the guests have informed us that Paris has quarrelled with his brother and sailed to Greece, the action follows him, and the third scene opens with Paris and Helen singing in ecstatic melismata.

Once again the sound-world signals the change: Paris's oboe is there, of course, here reaching its most expressive and decorative; henceforth it will lose its charm and influence, adding only acerbity to the war machines of the second act and absent altogether from the third. Helen's motif introduces a pair of flutes lusciously intertwined:

[5]

At the mention of Menelaus, Helen's husband, the clarinet completes the woodwind trio with a theme as elaborate as Paris's own. Now it is the turn of Paris to make his fateful decision, whether or not to elope with Helen, and bring an inevitable war upon Greece and Troy. He appeals to Zeus for guidance in an arioso that carries a string accompaniment of almost baroque cast. It is Hermes — 'Divine go-between, that's who I am' — who brings Zeus's response; he is announced by the 'death' motif (Example 2) and fragments of it punctuate his message as he orders Paris to award an apple to the most beautiful of the three Graces: Athene, goddess of wisdom, Hera, queen of the gods, and Aphrodite, goddess of love. The three goddesses speak with the tones of the opera's three female protagonists, and promise characteristic rewards; they are also accompanied by their characteristic musics. Athene is identified with Hecuba and her urgent violin line, while Hera introduces for the first time the extended cello recitative that will begin the third act and Andromache's prescient elegy:

[6]

Aphrodite has Helen's pair of flutes, and her eloquently understated call of Paris's name leaves him with little choice; he yields to love, awards the apple to Aphrodite and the act ends with the death motif expanded into a brittle toccata for piano and xylophone against grinding martial brass.

The second act plunges into the middle of war. The softening influence of the strings is discarded; they do not play at all, and everything is hard edges, brass, woodwind, percussion and an important role for the piano, save for the extended lyrical idyll which lies at its core, where a solo guitar is the single tone colour. Timpani and piano bring up the curtain on Hector and Paris on the walls of Troy. Hector is given a positive musical image for the first time, a brutal trombone motif that defines his brash machismo:

Paris has now been stripped of his obvious allure; when Hector eventually taunts him into answering the accusations of cowardice he does so to a new woodwind theme, satirically four-square, to which the oboe adds the timbre of things past, as if Tippett, even in the midst of battle, cannot deprive Paris of all the trappings of beauty:

[8] PARIS

(♩ = c.138)

Josephine Veasey as Andromache and Forbes Robinson as Priam in the 1962 Covent Garden première (photos: Houston Rogers, Theatre Museum)

To the rough and tumble of his sons' quarrel Priam's arrival and the reappearance of his theme bring momentary stability and a slight broadening of the hectic pace, though the relief is only temporary. The three-note motif of falling semitones with octave displacements derived from Priam's theme, which has run through the scene, returns: Hector goes back to the fighting, followed eventually by Paris. Brass and timpani introduce the first of this act's interludes in which the Old Man, still with the low woodwind in attendance, urges Hermes and his accompanying piccolo and high clarinet to magic him into the midst of the Greek camp and into the tent of Achilles.

In Achilles's extended lament for his homeland Tippett at last introduces an important element previously absent from this score. If anyone had doubted that his newly honed dramatic technique did not have the wherewithal to match a genuine lyric impulse, 'O rich-soiled land' decisively confounds them. Here, at the very heart of the opera, is a magnificent sustained set-piece which stands in sharp relief to the shorter-breathed declamation which surrounds it:

[9]

Equally no instrumental timbre could make a more pointed contrast with the warring trumpets that frame the scene than a guitar, and the music for Achilles's friend Patroclus is similarly restrained — a lachrymose cor anglais answered by a pair of horns. When Patroclus persuades Achilles to allow him to fight Hector the mood changes; the uncompromising piano returns with xylophone, cymbals and more aggressive horns, the chorus's warring cries are heard again. The act is moving towards a fierce, perfectly plotted climax; even the interlude for Hermes and the Old Man is hurried and overwhelmed by the sounds of battle.

The third scene begins sombrely: Hermes tells Priam of Patroclus's brave gesture over a dark-hued brooding passage for bassoons, horns and piano which peters out in an unadorned solo for timpani. Only when Paris arrives with the news that Hector has killed Patroclus does the return of his second-act theme (Example 8) bring even the semblance of light relief, and that of a painfully artificial, haunted kind. Hector's triumphant entry in Achilles's armour does nothing to lift the increasing desperation of the scene, as the action rushes towards ever greater tragedy. Hector leads his father and brother into a canonic thanksgiving to Zeus over the body of Patroclus, and the insertion of this almost reflex ritual — the opera's first true ensemble, to be balanced by the women's trio which will begin the third act — serves only to heighten the drama as the vocal lines become ever more intense and intertwined. At the climax of this solemn communion Achilles, roused to arms by the death of Patroclus, interrupts with his terrifying war cry, and this is taken up by the offstage chorus as the curtain falls. Tippett shapes the entire act towards this brilliant *coup de théâtre*.

There are no strings and no women to be heard in the second act of *Priam*; as if to emphasise a return to an essentially private world, the third begins with the sound of a solo cello (Example 6), which introduces Andromache, and with the appearance in turn of the three royal ladies of Troy, each launching a monologue that states her predicament. Andromache herself fears for Hector's safety in a stately, measured aria which moves in smooth lines; Hecuba reasserts her sense of selfless duty, her violin line now more fractured and agitated. Helen enters not to the pair of flutes of her love-struck past, but to a subdued string chord with only a brief harp flourish. Yet, goaded by the other women, she embarks upon a dramatic scena of unexpected breadth and intensity, which gradually becomes more elaborate and virtuosic as she reminds them of her conception as daughter of Leda and of Zeus disguised as a swan. Here the accompaniment of harp and piano gives way to divided strings as Helen recalls the beating of the swan's wings. Her defiance sets off a trio for the women which balances that for the men that closed Act Two, and one whose opening surely shows the influence of 'From the gutter' in Benjamin Britten's *Peter Grimes*:

71

The subsequent interlude is taken by Andromache's serving women over an athletic double-bass line; the first entry of the wind in Act Three introduces Priam alone. When the news of Hector's death prompts the king into a guilt-ridden monologue, echoing his aria of decision in Act One, scene one, it becomes obvious that this final act is to be constructed of substantial set pieces, in direct contrast to its predecessors. Priam's attempt to rationalise his grief is heightened by visions of the Nurse, Young Guard and Old Man — the Chorus from the first act — and by remembrances of its music. From Priam's despair the second interlude transports the action via a unison impassioned string line to Achilles in his tent, still introduced by the guitar, and now visited by Priam who begs for the body of Hector in the opera's most expressive aria:

[11] PRIAM

(♩ = c.76)

When Achilles invites Priam to drink to both their deaths they do so to an accented woodwind theme which acquires an almost surreal intensity as the scene develops to its climax, when Achilles tells Priam that he will be killed by Neoptolemus, Achilles's son.

In the final interlude Hermes, now the undisguised messenger of death, yet paradoxically without the death motif of his earlier appearances, comes to announce Priam's imminent death and to launch the opera's final lyrical effusion, a hymn to Music wafted over a tissue of flute, harp and piano:

[12] HERMES

(♩ = c.72)

Such an evocation of eternal renewal when Priam's position is quite hopeless runs a great dramatic risk: Tippett saves his most frank lyricism for this moment yet uses it to focus attention upon Priam when he threatens to be swept aside, his personal tragedy unnoticed in the tumult of events. It serves, perhaps, to prepare the audience for Priam's single visionary moment immediately before he is killed — 'I see mirrors myriad upon myriad moving the dark forms of creation' — a sudden apprehension of an inner life which little else in the opera prefigures.

Priam is seen before an altar receiving Paris to the background of an amalgam of earlier themes. The three women approach in turn each bringing her own thematic *alter ego*; Paris has one decision left to make before going to his death in the ruins of Troy: he admits Helen to Priam's presence, her feminine image restored and with it her dewy flute motif. There is a final remembrance of the death motif (Example 2) punctuated by Priam's final gnomic utterance. Neoptolemus kills the king to a barrage of wind and percussion; then, after a silence, percussion and a handful of strings offer the briefest of codas. Its three detached phrases are, says Tippett, 'our tears for Priam'.

King Priam

An Opera in Three Acts by Michael Tippett

Libretto by Michael Tippett

Dedicated to Karl Hawker

King Priam was first performed at the Coventry Festival (later at Covent Garden) on May 29, 1962.

Forbes Robinson as King Priam in the 1962 Covent Garden première (photo: Donald Southern)

CHARACTERS *in the scenes*

Priam *King of Troy*	*bass-baritone*
Hecuba *his wife*	*dramatic soprano*
Hector *their eldest son*	*baritone*
Andromache *Hector's wife*	*lyric dramatic soprano*
Paris *Priam's second son*	*boy soprano / tenor*
Helen *wife to Menelaus of Sparta,*	*mezzo-soprano*
then wife in adultery to Paris	
Achilles *a Greek hero*	*heroic tenor*
Patroclus *his friend*	*light baritone*

CHARACTERS AND CHORUS *in the scenes and interludes*

Nurse	*mezzo-soprano*
Old Man	*bass*
Young Guard	*lyric tenor*
Hermes *messenger of the Gods*	*high light tenor*

Chorus of Huntsmen, Wedding Guests, Serving Women, etc.

Es möge uns das Schicksal *gönnen, dass wir das innere
Ohr von dem Munde der Seele nicht abwenden.*

May Fate *grant that we never turn our inner ear
away from our soul's lips.*

Note: The numbers in square brackets refer to Andrew Clements's music examples.

Act One

Heralds with trumpets. Trumpet fanfares. Echo of trumpets behind the scene. Trumpets and drums in the orchestra. Cries behind the scene. More trumpets and drums and echoes and cries, gaining in urgency, until with a sudden silence:

Scene One. *The cry of a child. A point of light on a cradle. A nurse comes to quieten the child. Hecuba comes.*

HECUBA

What is it, nurse?

NURSE

The child is restless, and will not be still.

HECUBA

Nor have I the peace of mind to mother him.
Where is King Priam?

Priam enters. [1]

PRIAM

You've called me, Hecuba.
You are unlike yourself and strangely worried.
Is it the child?

HECUBA

Oh, I am restless and unsure.

The child cries again.

Indeed, the baby has caught my mood! My dream disturbs me.
What has come to Hecuba, the proud and fearless, true wife for you in these troubled times? For I am suddenly afraid.
I fear the meaning of my dream.

PRIAM

Our wise old man comes now to read it and advise. [1]
This mood of fear will pass.
Though I'm yet young, I've found that once the unknown is known, the way ahead is clear.
You will be strong and sure again. You will see.

HECUBA

Your shining confidence, on which all Troy depends!
It's good to hear it spoken.

PRIAM
(*going to look in the cradle*)

Even the child responds.

Old Man of Troy, you're welcome. The Queen is troubled by her dream. It will not leave her.
Is there a hidden meaning there?
That is her fear. Fear of the unknown; for I cannot read the messages from dreams.
We turn to you.
Yours is the cool head where knowledge and advice are stored like honey in the comb.
Wise man, unravel the Queen's dream.

OLD MAN
(*slowly*)

The dream means that Paris, this child, will cause as by an inexorable fate his father's death. [2]

The shock is so great that time seems to stand still for a moment.

HECUBA
(*crying out*)

Then am I no longer mother to this child. [3]
Troy and the city's king are sacred.
How could I have been so weak before?
Now I am strong again, and I know I shall never fail you further.
As Priam's mate I bore already Hector and can swear I shall bear Priam many sons.
Harsh though it is, I say, let this child be killed.

A short silence.

OLD MAN

What says King Priam?

PRIAM

A father and a King. [4]

He turns to the cradle.

So was I once a baby, born without choice.
So might I, his father, have been rejected by my parents, to be killed. But then, this child would not have been born. He is born because I lived. Shall he die that I may live?
A father and a King.
O child who cannot choose to live or die, I choose for you.

He turns from the cradle.

The Queen is right. [3]
Let the child be killed.

He signs for a young guard to take the child. Hecuba and Priam go out as the royal pair. As the guard moves towards the cradle, the child cries again. The guard stoops to pick it up, and goes. The Old Man and the Nurse come down to the footlights. By some easily manipulated change of dress, or by a mask perhaps, or a gesture, they can become a commenting Chorus. When speaking as Chorus they declaim; when speaking as expressive of the roles they do not declaim.

First Interlude.

NURSE AND OLD MAN (CHORUS)

Thus shall a story begin.
A child is born without choice.

OLD MAN

From its parents alone it lives.

NURSE

As now from its parents it dies.

YOUNG GUARD (ROLE)
(taking his place beside the others)

That is a crime.

NURSE (ROLE)

Ah!

OLD MAN (ROLE)

What is a crime?

YOUNG GUARD

To kill one's own child is a crime.

OLD MAN

It may be a duty.
Nature has many children for a man.
Priam is young and lusty, Hecuba healthy.
What means one child when the choice
involves the whole city?

YOUNG GUARD

How could a young man know enough to
dare to make such a choice?

OLD MAN

After the wise man read the dream, Priam
knew all. Priam made the choice that a king
would have to. Husband to Hecuba and
King of Troy, how other could he act?

NURSE

There are things left out of your science.
I had other apprehensions when the dream
was read.

OLD MAN AND YOUNG GUARD (CHORUS)

Time alone will tell.
We shall judge from the story.

YOUNG GUARD AND NURSE (CHORUS)

For life is a story from birth to death.

ALL

Scene will change into scene before you;
time rolling with each scene away.
Thus we follow the story.

OLD MAN

And the story of Priam shows that the
father-king, who made the bitter choice to
destroy a son, was favoured at first in home
and land. Hector grew to a fine lad, and
now there are other sons. The city calm and
flourishing; occasion for hunting and the
arts of peace.

Scene Two. *Priam and Hector, as a youth, and a few Huntsmen enter.*

FIRST HUNTSMAN

The bull is away over there. But the hounds
will hold it.

HECTOR

Father, you stay here, while I show you my
skill.

Hector runs out. Priam and the men watch his movements.

PRIAM

Troy will one day be proud of Hector.

FIRST HUNTSMAN

Look there! He has called the hounds to
heel and will meet the bull head on.

SECOND AND THIRD HUNTSMEN

Give him a cheer!

HUNTSMEN

Ohé! Ohé!

PRIAM
(still watching intently)

The bull is swerving. Hector, Hector, take
care!

SECOND HUNTSMAN

But there's another boy there —

THIRD HUNTSMAN

— sprung from nowhere!

SECOND HUNTSMAN

Look there!

THIRD HUNTSMAN

— Jumped on the bull's back —

FIRST HUNTSMAN

— and is riding away with the hounds after
him.

PRIAM
(turning from watching)

Fetch that boy to me. All of you.

The Huntsmen run off. Hector comes back.

76

HECTOR

How did that happen? Could you see?

PRIAM

There was a god or devil in that boy.
No boy unaided surpasses Hector.

He is again watching the chase offstage.

They have caught the bull and lost the boy.
(to Hector)
Stay here while I go.

*Priam goes after the Huntsmen. Hector
takes his place to watch. A pause. Paris, a
beautiful boy, younger than Hector, enters
from the other side. Hector turns to see him.
A slight pause.*   [5]

PARIS

They have taken my bull.

HECTOR

We want it for the games.

PARIS

He was my best friend.

HECTOR

You are friends with a bull!

PARIS

I have no playmates. I live alone with my
shepherd father.

HECTOR

Did he give you the bull, and teach you that
skill in riding?

PARIS

I've always ridden so. The bull is mine
because I ride him.
On his back one day I'll ride out into the
wide world.

HECTOR

Where will you go?

PARIS

I shall go first to Troy to take my place with
the young heroes.

HECTOR

To do that you must learn to drive horses
and chariots; but I could teach you.

PARIS

Who are you then?

HECTOR

I am from Troy.

PARIS

Are you a young hero?

HECTOR

Oh yes.

PARIS

And I will be a hero too.
Can I go back with you to Troy?

HECTOR

That depends on your father.

PARIS

He will let me go, I know, if you'll take me.

HECTOR

Then we must ask *my* father.

PARIS

Who is your father?

HECTOR

He comes now. He is King Priam.

*Priam enters with the Huntsmen. He looks
fixedly for a while at Paris.*   [5]

Father, he's a shepherd boy.
He wants to come to Troy to be a young
hero.
I would like to have him with us.

PRIAM

Beloved Hector, if you want him — and
Troy has need of heroes.
But does his father wish it? He's not of age
to go without consent.

PARIS

Oh, my father will consent. That's what he
promised.

PRIAM

Do you really choose to leave your father
and this country life? To live in barracks
and be trained in fighting?

PARIS

I love my father and my home, but I want
adventure.
I choose, I choose the life in Troy.
For I belong to Troy, I know.

PRIAM

What is your name, boy?

PARIS

Paris.

*A moment's silence. Priam's mind and the
music go back to Scene One. Priam comes
down stage; while Hector, Paris and the
Huntsmen move back.*   [2]

PRIAM

So I'd often hoped it might be;
that accident or god reversed the choice,

sometime between my order to the guard
and its fulfilment.
So indeed it must be.
For my heart knows here is my second son.
What now? What now?
I have a deepening anguish.
If it was a crime, those years ago, to crush
the natural life, the father's love, because
one is a King, what now?
What now?
Do I now with my own hands that failed to
kill a child, kill the boy,
Because he chooses with the certainty of
youth to come to Troy,
Because he may fulfil the augury,
Because he is my son?
I have a deepening anguish.
Where are the shadows from the past who
haunt my dreams;

*The Nurse, Old Man, Young Guard are
present.*

Who know there was a real dream of
Hecuba's that cannot be undreamt?
                    (*to the Nurse*)
You nursed the child for Hecuba too
troubled by her dream.
                    (*to the Old Man*)
You read the dream's meaning and foretold
my fate.
                    (*to the Young Guard*)
You took the child to kill it, but in sudden
pity gave it to a shepherd. Actors in-
dissolubly bound with me to play a crucial
scene.
Now it has come again.
Now I must choose afresh.
Now, in the moment of recognition,
Now with Zeus's help,
Now — you shall see a less ignoble man.
For I accept the trick of fate that saved my
son, and what he, Paris, chooses I uphold.
Let it mean my death!

OLD MAN

Do you speak for Troy as for yourself?

PRIAM

Yes! I speak for Troy as well.

*Priam and the Huntsmen go off back-stage
with Hector and Paris.*

Second Interlude.

NURSE, OLD MAN AND YOUNG GUARD
(CHORUS)

Ah, but life is a bitter charade.
We go from birth to death, but nothing is
plain.
Perhaps at the end, a glimmering of sense, a
residue of meaning.
(We shall see from the story.)
But on the way there,

Ah, life is a bitter charade,
Without and within a complex knot, that
never unties,
Though sometimes cut with a rending
sound,
The orators drowned by a scream of pain.
Ah, life is a bitter charade.
Now the role will change from boy to youth.
'The force that through the green fuse
drives the flower'
Body draws body to a destined bed.
Yet we act in a dream.
Ah, but life is a bitter charade.

        Wedding Guests from Troy enter.

MALE WEDDING GUESTS (ROLE)

There, look there!
We could have guessed it!
Droning yourselves into a coma.
Too fussed with meanings and morals, to
live from the moment like us.

FEMALE WEDDING GUESTS (ROLE)

And what you've missed in Troy!
Yes, Hector's sumptuous wedding to
Andromache.
The bride pure and beautiful in white.

MEN

Very dignified, every inch a princess.

WOMEN

Hector in a green embroidered tunic, with
golden buckles.

MEN

The band of young heroes on parade.

WOMEN

Hector, the bravest of them all.

MEN

Hector, Troy's champion.

MEN AND WOMEN

Hector, Troy's champion!

WOMEN

Yet a man for a home;
A woman's ideal.

YOUNG GUARD

And how did young Paris take the wedding?

A MALE GUEST

He did not like it at all. The truth is, once
they knew they were brothers, Hector and
Paris never got on.

ANOTHER MALE GUEST

Upsetting to Priam, but it's only natural.

OLD MAN

And so?

MALE WEDDING GUESTS (CHORUS)

So Paris has now left Troy, scorning his
father, and sailed to Greece.

FEMALE WEDDING GUESTS (CHORUS)

Where Menelaus keeps open house at
Sparta with his wife,

MEN

Daughter of Zeus,

MEN AND WOMEN

Queen Helen.

Scene Three. *As from an inner room, the
voices of Helen and Paris off stage singing a
melisma. Helen and Paris come from the
inner room.* [6]

PARIS

Helen!

HELEN

Paris!

PARIS

Are you woman or witch that you enchant
me so?

HELEN

I am Helen.

PARIS

And I am Paris:
Young and strong with desire when you are
near.

HELEN

I must go.

PARIS

Go?

HELEN

To Menelaus.

PARIS

Helen! After such love with me can you go
now to lie with Menelaus?

HELEN

He is my husband.

PARIS

What does that mean? You fear to refuse
him though you've ceased to love him?

HELEN

He is my husband. I may not deny him.

PARIS

Then I must share you?
No!
You must choose between us, Helen.
Come with me to Troy. Or stay with him.
Which shall it be?

HELEN

How can I choose?
I must stay with him. Or go with you.
I cannot tell.

PARIS

If I'm forced to sail away, will you come
with me?

HELEN

You will be forced to sail away — at dawn.

PARIS

At dawn! Forced? By whom?

HELEN

Menelaus.

PARIS

Then Helen, will you come with me?

No answer.

Helen?

HELEN

Paris.

PARIS

Will you come with me?

HELEN

If you fetch me, I will come.

She goes out.

PARIS

If I fetch her, she will come.
O Helen, you leave me to the moment so
desired and feared.
Carried on the wind of love, if I carry you
away; another's wife! A city's Queen! Who
will escape the avenging war? [7]
O Helen, Helen, can we choose that?
You will answer Helen: do we choose at all
when our divided bodies rush together as
though halves of one?
We love.
O Gods, why give us bodies with such
power of love, if love's a crime?
Is there a choice at all?
Answer, father Zeus, divine lover!
Answer.

Hermes appears as Chorus. [2]

HERMES (ROLE)

Divine go-between, that's who I am:
Hermes the messenger.

I run errands for the gods and goddesses.
I bring a message from Zeus.

(CHORUS)

'To Paris, the most beautiful man alive.
You are to choose between three Graces:
Athene, Hera, Aphrodite. You shall give
this apple to the most beautiful.'

*Hermes gives Paris the apple, who takes it as
in a dream. The Goddesses appear: Hecuba
as Athene, Andromache as Hera, Helen as
Aphrodite. All are young.*

PARIS

I dream, I dream!

*Paris walks up and down and observes them.
Then he comes to Hermes.*

They are all beautiful. How can I choose
between them?

HERMES (ROLE)

Yet you must choose. By Zeus's command.

PARIS

How shall I give the apple to one, and
escape the wrath of the others?

HERMES

You will not escape. That is the law of life.

PARIS

What shall I do then?

HERMES

Go forward as a man must.
Ask what they offer you, should you honour
them.

Paris approaches Athene.

PARIS

Lady Athene, if I honour you, what is my
fate?

ATHENE

Handsome are you, Paris, and you are
brave.   [3]
I will inspire you on the battlefield.
Troy will be grateful if you honour me.

PARIS
(*rudely*)

You speak like my mother Hecuba.

*He turns away and crosses over towards
Hera.*

Lady Hera, if I honour you, what is my
reward?

HERA

You are brave, Paris, and you are good.   [8]
You cannot live always on the battlefield.
I will give that warmth and trust within the
marriage bond that is man's best reward, if
you honour me.

PARIS
(*with exasperation*)

You speak like my brother's wife,
Andromache.

He returns to Hermes.

They have nothing to offer.

HERMES

There is still a third.

Paris approaches Aphrodite.

PARIS

Aphrodite, if I honour you, what will you
promise me?
                    A long silence.
Well?
                    Another silence.
Will you not speak, O Goddess of all love
that is desire?

APHRODITE

Paris!   [6]

PARIS
(*involuntarily*)

Helen!

APHRODITE

Paris!

PARIS

O Aphrodite, shall I honour you?

HERA

Stay, Paris, stay. For if you steal another's
wife, then I will curse you.

ATHENE

Consider Sparta's hurt pride. If you dis-
honour Hera, there will come war that
pities no man.   [3]

APHRODITE

Paris!   [6]

Paris gives Aphrodite the apple.

HERA AND ATHENE

Accursed! Accursed!

PARIS
(*shouting*)

You are phantoms.
I will fetch Helen and she will come.
To Troy!

Paris rushes out. The Goddesses disappear.

HERMES

To Troy!

                    Curtain.

Act Two

Scene One. *Hector appears in armour upon or beside the walls of Troy, with Paris unarmed.*

HECTOR

So you've given up fighting!   [9]
I'm not surprised.
You're mad about women, you pretty boy;
and for myself I wish you'd never lived.
What can the Greeks think we are, when
the second son of Troy, Prince handsome
Paris, turns coward?
Is really this the man who stole a wife from
Menelaus?
You had a chance, an hour back in battle
with the avenging Greeks, to meet the
husband face to face.
You failed it, as you did at Sparta; turned
the back and ran away.
Where to? What for?
To go to Helen.

PARIS

Hector, you may be right to call me
names.   [10]
Yet I wish you were not so like a living
hammer.
You tire me.
And once for all, my good looks are my
birthright, to be envied not despised.
I ran away from Menelaus I know; and
Helen is angry.
But I fight as well as any Trojan after you.

HECTOR

Then fight!
Or must we wait till Helen taunts you, you
woman-struck seducer?

Priam enters.

PRIAM

Stop wrangling, sons! Let the Greeks
quarrel, but not Troy.   [1]
I chide as father, and command as King.
The camp of Greeks is split wide open:
Wrath of Achilles against King
Agamemnon for a girl.
So sharp the quarrel, Achilles has now
drawn apart with all his men, and will not
fight.
Troy should instantly attack.

HECTOR

Agreed. And would my brother fight we'd
drive the Greeks into the sea.   [9]

PRIAM

Go Paris now and arm. Hector will wait
here.   [1]

    Paris goes.

HECTOR

I tell you, father, but I'm filled with shame.
He may be man enough to man a woman —
his good looks see to that — but he's not
man enough to fight. He ran away from
Menelaus there in front of all. I wish you'd
never got him; or had really strangled him
at birth.

PRIAM

Calm yourself, Hector. Those are words I
will not hear.
We need now every son I have. Turn your
anger to the Greeks; let Paris be.

HECTOR

Do you reproach me that I love the Greeks,
Troy's enemies?
O father!
But Menelaus, enemy, commands more
honour than Paris, brother.
Where is he now? I stay no more.

Hector strides off. Men's voices in the distance: War! War!

PRIAM

So Trojans honour Menelaus more than
Paris.
As many Greeks set Hector now above
Achilles.
Do I pretend?
Oh, vain to vex the mind in time of war.
Vital alone that Paris learns to fight before
Achilles regains his manhood.
    (calling)
Paris! Paris!

    Paris comes in armour.

PARIS

Has Hector gone already? Yet I'm swift
enough to catch him.

He goes off running. Men's voices off stage: War! War!

PRIAM

My sons united!
Let them be ruthless!
But, O Apollo, bring beloved Hector back
to me triumphant —
    (trumpets)
— and may the Greeks stay broken!

Drums: which continue through the Interlude. Priam goes.

First Interlude.

OLD MAN (ROLE)

Hermes! Hermes with the winged feet, come quick!

Hermes comes.

HERMES (ROLE)

Old phantom tied to Troy, what do you need from the god who's tied to nothing?

OLD MAN

When I first knew the avenging Greeks would come,
Agamemnon and dazzling Achilles, my heart failed me.
Now my heart exults.
Take me, Hermes, through the Greek camp, unseen, to spy into that tent and gloat for Troy upon Achilles sulking.

HERMES

Gloat not too soon. Dazzling Achilles has a heart that one man reaches.
You shall truly see into that tent, when we have crossed the plain, deaf to the din of battle.

While they cross the plain towards the Greek ships, the sound of men's cries off stage, drums and trumpets etc., grows to a climax, which stops as Achilles is seen in the tent with Patroclus.

Scene Two.

ACHILLES
(singing to a lyre)   [11]

O rich-soiled land of Phthia
Where we grew to manhood
You and I, Patroclus;
Shall we tread
After the war
The homeland again?

Oh, there still lives my father,
With Neoptolemus my son.
(You loved him, Patroclus.)
Shall we kiss,
After the war,
My tall son again?

Patroclus, who has been sitting with his head in his hands, is now visibly sobbing.

Why are you weeping, Patroclus, like a little girl needing her nurse?

PATROCLUS

Your song made me weep; to think of your father, our home and your son.

ACHILLES

Forget the song. It was sad.

PATROCLUS

Oh, I wept too for our comrades here before Troy; those who are wounded or dead. And for the waste of your manhood in this war.

ACHILLES

Do not provoke me, Patroclus.

PATROCLUS

Hard-hearted Achilles, from your insensate pride the Greeks will soon go down in defeat.

ACHILLES

Aha! So they now see what it is to misuse me. When we fought against Thebe, I was the first to enter the town. I killed Andromache's father and all his sons. I was given a girl as my prize. Till Agamemnon stole her (no other word) and the craven Greeks applauded. Is that fair dealings for Achilles?

PATROCLUS

You live for your quarrel.
(bitter)
Soon men may forget you can fight.
(taunting)
'Is Achilles really a hero?' they'll say.

ACHILLES

Patroclus, they would not dare!
Look on that shining armour, bronze and silver, which I keep ready till the Greeks come begging to Achilles, as they will. They cannot take Troy without me.

Cries of 'War!' off stage.

PATROCLUS

They may never take Troy.
Hector has reached our ships, and if he burns them, we may never see Greece again.

ACHILLES

Ah no! A check to the Greeks but not defeat.

More cries off stage.

The danger is grave. Yet I cannot give way.

PATROCLUS

Then let your armour go to fight.

ACHILLES

Meaning?

PATROCLUS

I am not you, Achilles, but disguise me in your shining armour, set me in your chariot with the immortal horses, I shall be you in all but body, and under your plume (though you stay here) can drive back the Trojans across the plain.

ACHILLES

Patroclus you shall!
The scheme is worthy of my fertile brain.
Arm yourself, Patroclus, now as me.

*Achilles helps Patroclus put on the armour.
Cries off stage. Achilles looks out of the tent
for a moment.*

Hector has fired the ships. We act in the
nick of time. More than my armour, I'll
lend you strength shouting my war-cry,
when the moment comes. You will drive all
before you.
But go no further than the open plain.
I must be first to enter Troy.

*Achilles goes to a chest to take out a silver
cup to make libation to Zeus. They come out
of the tent.*

All-powerful Zeus, I pray that Patroclus
may drive off the Trojans —
    (*a great blare of trumpets*)
— and come back safe to me here.

*He pours the libation. A terrific barrage of
drums; which then continue to beat until
Hector reappears before Priam.*

PATROCLUS

Achilles, dear lord Achilles, goodbye.

ACHILLES

Much loved Patroclus, goodbye.

*They embrace. Patroclus rushes away to the
beating of the drums.*

Second Interlude.

OLD MAN (ROLE)

Oh, what a threat to Troy!
Hermes, Hermes, what's to be done?

HERMES (ROLE)

Why ask me? I am not tied to Troy.

(CHORUS)

The gods rejoice when a hero like Achilles
chooses at last to redeem his virtue.

OLD MAN (ROLE)

I have no life beyond the bounds of Troy.
Help from the gods means help for Troy.
Return, Hermes, now at once and bring the
news to Priam.

HERMES (CHORUS)

The messenger is instantaneous when the
news is feared.
Priam will have guessed.

(ROLE)

But yet, since you ask, I will go again across
the field of battle.

Music for Hermes's return across the plain.

Scene Three. *Priam appears upon or
beside the walls of Troy. Hermes enters as a
messenger.*

HERMES
(*as though short of breath from running*)

A hero in Achilles's armour, perhaps
Patroclus, rushed headlong from the ships,
driving all before him.

PRIAM

So had I feared. It is Patroclus. He alone
could touch Achilles's heart.

HERMES
(*having regained his breath*)

But Hector and Paris have rallied all your
sons, and Hector fights Patroclus, man to
man.

Paris enters.

PARIS

Father, have you heard the news?   [10]

PRIAM

That Hector fights Patroclus, while you
run back!

PARIS

Oh, but Hector has already killed him.
Stripped the body.
You shall see Hector come resplendent in
Achilles's armour.

*Hermes has gone. Hector enters in Achilles's
armour.*

HECTOR

All Trojans, all fought bravely and together
till Achilles sent Patroclus into battle. But
with Apollo's help I, Hector, killed Achilles's
comrade and wear Achilles's armour now
as mine.
Father Priam, and you too brother Paris,
before I go to greet Andromache and kiss
my son, let us give thanks to Zeus.

PRIAM, HECTOR AND PARIS
(*singing together, but with Hector leading*)

O Zeus, King of all gods and goddesses;
High on Olympus you have bowed your
head
For death to the Greek hero, to Patroclus;
Glorious victory to Hector, and to Troy.
And O Apollo (who fights for us)
When the goddesses and gods besiege
Zeus's ear,
Speak first and loudest to ensure
The Olympian head bows once again to
uphold our walls,
And twice to destroy their ships.

*At the height of the ensemble, with Priam,
Hector and Paris facing the audience at the
footlights, Achilles appears before the tent to*

deliver his war-cry, a bloodcurdling melisma that echoes round the stage. Hector stands as though transfixed.

OLD MAN
(*in between the tent and the walls, gloating over the naked body of Patroclus on the ground*)

Achilles's war cry!

Achilles delivers the cry a second time.

PRIAM
O Hector!

OLD MAN
O Troy!

Achilles delivers the cry a third time.

Quick Curtain.

Achilles (Neil Jenkins) sends Patroclus (John Hancorn) out to fight in his place in the 1984 Kent Opera production by Nicholas Hytner, designed by David Fielding (photo: Roger de Wolf)

Act Three

Scene One. *Andromache alone on the stage. A Serving Woman comes. Other Serving Women wait with a cauldron.* [8]

SERVING WOMAN

Lady Andromache, should we not light the fire?

ANDROMACHE

Yes. Prince Hector will want his bath the moment he comes from fighting.

The Serving Women go.

Do I deceive myself?
There is foreboding in the heart and in the home, as on the day Achilles killed my father and my brothers.
Was that not enough, that now today he wants my husband?
Husbands are worth more than comrades.
Yet Achilles claims my Hector for Patroclus; 'death for death'; in which equation the most brutal wins.
Rouse Achilles he becomes a brute insatiate, out of range of human frailty or human pity.
Hector remains to the end (ah!) but a man.
My love is open,
While I mask my fear.

Hecuba comes.

HECUBA

Daughter Andromache, you must go out now on the walls to plead with Hector to come inside the city, for he is there alone to face Achilles. Deaf to Priam, he will attend to you. Hector must be brought within, for the sake of Troy! [3]

ANDROMACHE
(crying out)

For the sake of Troy!
O Gods, is there no other sake?
What of Hector my husband?
What of Hector our son's father?
Intolerable!
I will not beg my husband from the walls of Troy. My place is here in my home.

HECUBA

And what will be your home if Troy is taken?
When Hector and all our men are dead, you will be given, stubborn as you are, as slave to a Greek. That is the price of pride that will not appeal to Hector in a public street.

ANDROMACHE

Are you not stubborn too?
Go now to your husband, to Priam, and beg him deliver Helen to the avenging Greeks. Then Troy — and Hector — will be safe on the instant.

HECUBA

Daughter, you are a fool.
No war is fought for a woman.
If, because of Helen, the Greeks landed from their thousand ships, it is Troy they want, not Helen.

Helen enters. A moment's silence.

ANDROMACHE

Did you hear? The war is not for you at all.
You are wanted neither here nor there.

HELEN

Your words are meaningless to me, if bitter.
My husband Paris wishes me to visit you.
He says —

ANDROMACHE

'My husband Paris.' Listen to that!
Your husband Menelaus. There is where you belong.
What of your marriage vows to Menelaus?
Did you not feel the sacred ties of home?
Oh, but you cannot. A wife is other than a whore.
Not love drew you to Paris, but lust.
Where did he learn his lovers' tricks?
From other whores before you.

HECUBA

Control yourself, Andromache, insults are out of place.

ANDROMACHE

Let me finish!
(to Helen)
Go back to Greece, adulteress, and let this war be stopped.

HECUBA

It will not stop. Calm yourself and know your duty.

HELEN

Let her rave. I, Helen, am untouched.
She cannot know me, what I am.
Once, as I came along the walls, the old men spoke of me, for so I heard:
'No wonder Greeks and Trojans go to war for such a woman.' And they spoke well.

For I am Zeus's daughter, conceived when
the great wings beat above Leda.   [12]
Women like you, wives and mothers, cannot
know what men may feel with me.
You talk of lust and whoring, your words
glance off such truth of love whose tempest
carried Ganymede into the sky.
What can it be that throbs in every nerve,
beats in the blood and bone, down through
the feet into the earth, then echoed by the
stars?
Intolerable desire, burning ecstasy.
All prices paid, all honour lost in this
bewilderment.
Immortal, incommensurable,
Love such as this stretches up to heaven, for
it reaches down to hell.

HECUBA

Oh, that my ears should hear impiety so
gross!
Must Troy become a burning hell to salve
your vanity?
Why was I once so weakened by a dream?
Had I but smothered Paris at birth, you
would not be here in Troy.

*Hecuba and Helen stare at one another as
they realise the gulf opening between them.*

ANDROMACHE
(turning away)

O Hector, our few years of home end in a
cruel bitter fate unwilled by us. Husband,
take my loving with you to the grave.

The three women sing together. [13]

HECUBA

Woman to Goddess,
I to you Athene,
Pray for strength
That heroes may endure,
The city stand.
And to my man, King
Priam of towered Troy,
Grant balm of comfort,
From the steadfast mate.
For death draws near.
Goddess to me, woman,
Grant but this.

ANDROMACHE

Woman to Goddess,
I to you, O Hera,
Pray for wives
And husbands and the home
Where children grow.
And to my man, horse-taming Hector, with
the flashing plume,
Grant balm of comfort,
That his life was pure.
For death draws near.
Goddess to me, woman,
Grant but this.

HELEN

Woman to Goddess,
I to Aphrodite,
Pray for lovers
And the divine madness
Of insatiable desire.
And to my man, beautiful Paris envied of
all,
Grant balm of comfort,
That he lay with Helen.
For death draws near.
Goddess to me, woman,
Grant but this.

ANDROMACHE

Now you shall go. I have forewarning from
within, quicker than the fastest runner
running here.
Hector is dead. Now you shall go.

HECUBA

O Troy! O Priam!

*Hecuba goes. Helen and Andromache look
proudly at each other before Helen goes. The
old Serving Woman comes to Andromache.*

SERVING WOMAN

The bath is hot. Will the Lord Hector
come?

ANDROMACHE

Yes. Yes. Yes.

*Andromache goes. The Serving Women
come down stage as a Chorus.*

First Interlude.

SERVING WOMEN (CHORUS)

No. No. No.
We have it from the runner who has
reached the house.
We always know.
Yet who are we?
Not the names that figure in the drama.
Un-named. Slaves. (Yes.) Slaves.
To whom the fate of towered Troy is but a
change of masters.
What else?
Rape! Death!
Are these Greek or Trojan?

They laugh.

Yet we could tell the story too, the pathetic
story of our masters.
Viewed from the corridor.

Cries off stage.

All the commotion now.
Would you know what that is?
News. News of Hector's shocking death
spreads like plague through Troy, from the
slave to the heroes, Priam's sons, and to the
Queen.

Only King Priam does not know.
For who shall tell him?
This news may break his heart or turn his mind.
Troy will crumble.
Who will tell him as he rages, rages in an inner room?
Look! There! He comes.

The Serving Women go off as Priam is seen alone.

Scene Two.

PRIAM
(alone)

What is happening?
Am I no longer King? Forced from the walls by my people, locked in my room.
Hecuba refusing to speak.
Something is known that I have not been told. O Gods!
(shouting)
Let me out! Let me out!

Answering shouts off stage.

VOICE OF PARIS
(off stage)

Unhand me, mother Hecuba.
I will see him.

Paris enters.

PARIS

Father.

PRIAM

Son.

PARIS

Prepare yourself, for you must know.

PRIAM

Yes, I must know.

PARIS

All are afraid, so I have come to tell you.

PRIAM

What?

PARIS

Your first and dearest son, the hero Hector —

PRIAM

Ah!

PARIS

Achilles has killed him, and shamefully misused him.

PRIAM

Say that again.

PARIS

Achilles has killed him, and shamefully misused him.

PRIAM
(suddenly bursting out)
And you have dared to come and tell me.
Courageous to tell a stricken father truth, afraid to fight.
Hector was a hero. You're but a playboy.
Why did *you* not kill Patroclus? Why did *you* not fight Achilles?
Oh, I could have spared you well for Hector; for Hector my son.
Are you my son? No.
Or if you are, would that I had strangled you at birth as the Old Man told me.

PARIS

What horror! What injustice!
You are mad for grief!
I am your son. I am no coward.
You will not see me more till I have killed Achilles, and avenged my brother.

Paris rushes off.

PRIAM
(moaning)

Oh! Oh! Oh!
A father and a King.   [4]
My death they said, but never Hector's.
Had they said Hector's, I would have killed the other in the cradle.
Oh yes I would. No doubt of it.

Young Guard and Old Man appear.

YOUNG GUARD (ROLE)

A crime.

OLD MAN (ROLE)

A duty.

PRIAM

Phantoms! Phantoms from the fatal hour.
Is not the present harsh enough, that you should come to mock me from the past?

YOUNG GUARD

Think on the present then.
What have you done to your son, Paris, now?

PRIAM

I have no son, Paris.
I had a son, Hector. But he is dead.
O Gods!

YOUNG GUARD

You engendered Paris. That cannot be shuffled off.

PRIAM

Let him avenge his brother then.

YOUNG GUARD

What is this vengeance? Recount.
Who killed Patroclus?

PRIAM

Great Hector, defending the city.

YOUNG GUARD

Who avenged Patroclus, killing Hector?

PRIAM

Barbaric Achilles. Curse him!

YOUNG GUARD

Who kills Achilles?

PRIAM

Paris —
> *A pause.*
— my son.

YOUNG GUARD

Who will kill Paris?

PRIAM

O Gods!

OLD MAN AND OFF STAGE MEN'S VOICES
> *(on a roll of drums)*

Agamemnon.

YOUNG GUARD

What then is this vengeance that you want?
> *A pause.*

PRIAM

I do not want these deaths. I want my own.
There was no truth in what the Old Man
said. O bitter disillusion! Twisted around
his finger,
Had he no pity for a young man's ignorance?
> *(to the Old Man)*
Your reading of the dream was false.

OLD MAN

No.

PRIAM

Hector's death, not mine.

OLD MAN

No.

PRIAM

You told me lies.

OLD MAN

I told you truth, so far I knew it.

PRIAM
> *(turning away)*

Why, why, why, why
Should this truth entrap us?
Toys, dupes, decoys of fate.

Never, never, never
Masters in the house.
> *(to the Old Man)*
Why? Answer! Why?

NURSE
> *(appearing)*

The soul will answer from where the pain is
quickest.

PRIAM

Where the pain is quickest. O Hector, my
son, my son.

> *A pause.*

NURSE

Where did Hector's death begin?

PRIAM

Where did Hector's death begin?
Not at conception, for I loved my wife, and
loved my child.
His death began at that fatal flaw of pity
that you —
> *(pointing to the Young Guard)*
— sensed in me.
I should have been hard like Hecuba.
Like this Old Man.
Then Hector would be here.

NURSE

One son to live only by another's death.
Is that the law of life you favour?

PRIAM

I favour nothing. But I answer:
Yes. Yes. Yes.

NURSE

Listen to your soul's echo.

VOICES
> *(off stage)*

No. No. No.

PRIAM

These things are tricks. I will hear no more.
I curse my parents that they got me.
I curse this life that has no meaning.
I curse my soul that will not let me rest.
Who dares to judge Priam, King of Troy?
Who dares to judge Priam, father of Hector,
father — and of that other son?
None would dare judge me, if my own soul
were still.
Therefore I curse the soul.
And I curse you, phantoms. Oh, I curse,
I curse.

> *Priam sinks to the ground.*

YOUNG GUARD AND OLD MAN

Lie there and judge yourself —   [4]

YOUNG GUARD

— father —

OLD MAN

— and King.

NURSE

Measure him time with mercy.

Second Interlude.

*The time is measured by an instrumental
interlude. The figures of Priam and the
Chorus fade away, and only darkness is left,
and moving shadows. When enough time is
measured by the music, a point of light grows
on the stage. It is . . .*

Scene Three. *Achilles at night in his tent.
The corpse of Hector is covered by a cloth.
Achilles sits brooding over the body. Priam
enters. Achilles starts up.* [11]

ACHILLES

Priam! Here! What is this?

He raises his head to call.

PRIAM

Do not call the guards. I am unarmed,
alone. Led by Hermes I am here; an old
man bringing gifts.

*Priam looks towards the corpse of Hector, as
though unable to control his trembling need
to touch it.*

A father come to ransom the body of his
son.

ACHILLES

Then you are mad, old man. Were you not a
father, old as my own father, I would kill
you now.
There is indeed the body of Hector. But
cruel though I am, I will not force you to
uncover it. It is mutilated shamefully, and
by my own hands. For this flesh is Hector's
and not —
And not — and never —
The living flesh of him I loved —
The gentle prince, Patroclus.

*Achilles sits down sobbing. Priam in a swift
movement, kneels before Achilles, clasps
Achilles's knees and kisses his hands.*

PRIAM

I clasp your knees, Achilles, and kiss your
terrible, man-slaying hands. [14]
Think on your father, Achilles, the lone old
man in Greece, waiting for you to return.
At least he still has you. While I, with
Hector dead, have nothing. Think on your
father. Remember the gods. Be merciful
before the dawn. For I have done what no

father did before. Kissed the hands of him
who killed my son.

*Achilles takes Priam's hands off his knees,
and lifts Priam's head.*

ACHILLES

Old man, I am touched. Brutal Achilles has
felt pity! You shall have the body to take
back to Troy.

Achilles stands up to pray.

Patroclus, do not be angry when you hear in
the dead lands, that I gave Priam Hector's
body back. You shall have your proper
share of the princely ransom I shall ask.
Farewell.

*Perhaps Achilles draws a curtain to shut the
corpse from view.*

Come, old father, you are tired and shall
stay here the night. Let us drink wine.

They sit at the table.

I drink to my death. The death of dazzling
Achilles.
Since I failed Patroclus I want only my
death.

PRIAM

I go to a different death, Achilles.

ACHILLES

I shall die first, and in battle.
Which of the Trojans will kill me?
Tell me that.

PRIAM

Paris will kill you. Paris, my son.

ACHILLES

And who will kill you, at the altar, King
Priam?
My goddess-mother told me, so I will tell
you.
Neoptolemus will kill you at the altar.
Neoptolemus, *my* son.

Third Interlude.

Hermes enters as messenger of death.

HERMES (CHORUS)

I come as messenger of death.
For the story will soon end.
A timeless music played in time.

(ROLE)
(*to the spectators*)

Do not imagine all the secrets of life can be
known from a story.
Oh, but feel the pity and the terror as Priam
dies.
He already breathes an air as from another
planet.

The world where he is going,
Where he has gone,
Cannot communicate itself through him,
(He will speak only to Helen in the end)
But through the timeless music.

(CHORUS)
He turns back to the altar again.

O divine music,   [15]
O stream of sound,
In which the states of soul
Flow, surfacing and drowning,
While we sit watching from the bank
The mirrored world within, for
'Mirror upon mirror mirrored is all the
show.'
O divine music,
Melt our hearts,
Renew our love.

*Sudden eruption of Scene Four as Hermes
goes.*

Scene Four. *Before an altar. Paris, dishev-
elled from fighting.*

PARIS

Where is my father? Where is Priam?

Priam enters slowly.

PRIAM

What is it now?

PARIS

I have killed Achilles, and avenged Hector.
Embrace me, father.

PRIAM

You ask too much.

PARIS

Well then I offer, for you are still my father,
I will take you and Helen, and leave the
doomed city to found another Troy.

PRIAM

You are not the founding sort.
Nor will I go.
Stay to defend me till I am ready. Keep all
away.

*Priam goes to the altar and turns his back on
Paris. Cries off stage as Hecuba comes on
and meets Paris.*

HECUBA

The Greeks are in the city. All is lost. Why
are you not in the fight?   [3]

PARIS

I obey my father to defend him, while he
prays.

HECUBA

Too late for prayer. Let him kiss his wife
goodbye.

PARIS

Stay here. I will call him.

Paris goes to Priam at the altar.

It is my mother and your wife.

Priam turns to Paris.

PRIAM

I cannot see her.

*He turns back to the altar again. Paris comes
back to Hecuba.*

HECUBA

Changed and distraught.

PARIS

He prays.

HECUBA

Let him pray the Greeks will spare your
youngest brother, still a child, when all the
Trojan men and you are slain. Enslaved in
the Greek lands, Hecuba will remember
proud Troy.

Hecuba goes. Cries off stage.

PARIS

Father, shall I go now defend my mother?

Priam does not answer. Andromache comes.

ANDROMACHE
(*to Paris*)

Out of my way, adulterer, that I may go to
Priam.

PARIS

I guard him as he prays.

ANDROMACHE

You will have need to guard him!
For though you killed Achilles (too late! too
late!)
Achilles's son is raging through the town
swinging my own dead child as club.

*Paris hides his face for a moment, then goes
to Priam.*

PARIS

It is my sister and your son's wife.

PRIAM
(*turning to Paris*)

I cannot see her.

*He turns back to the altar. Paris comes
towards Andromache, but she is already
going, withdrawn and dignified. She does
not look at Helen, when they pass, as Helen
comes.*

PARIS

Helen!

90

HELEN

Paris! [6]

There is a long silence. They stand silent together, the beautiful, ill-fated pair. Paris goes to Priam at the altar.

PARIS

It is your daughter, and my wife.
It is Helen.

PRIAM
(turning to Paris)

Go, my son, to find a hero's death in burning. Let Helen come to me.

Paris goes. As Helen comes towards Priam, the trumpets and drums and cries from the Prelude to Act One return, with ever increasing urgency. Troy is already burning.

PRIAM

Mysterious daughter, who are you?

HELEN

I am Helen.

PRIAM

Have I been gentle with you?

HELEN

Neither you, nor Hector, ever by word or deed reproached me.

PRIAM

Why was that, I wonder? Why do I speak gently now, below the screams of the dying, as the city burns?

HELEN

I cannot tell. I am Helen.

PRIAM

You loved Paris. He is already dead.

HELEN

Yes.

PRIAM

You will go back to Greece.

HELEN

Yes.

PRIAM

For you are Helen.

Priam kisses Helen. Helen goes. The trumpets are now exacerbated to the extreme. Priam sinks down before the altar, and tries to say something, but cannot be heard above the din. As his lips continue to move soundlessly, Hermes appears as a God. The din suddenly ceases. In the moment of tranquility Priam can just be heard. He has lifted himself up, but his eyes are closed.

I see mirrors, [2]
Myriad upon myriad moving
The dark forms
Of creation.

Hermes descends to Hades. The din breaks out again as Achilles's son, with other Greeks, bursts onto the stage and runs his sword through Priam at the altar, who dies instantly. Complete silence for a moment. Everyone stock still. A few bars of music.

Curtain.

'He will speak only to Helen in the end': Anne Mason as Helen and Rodney Macann as Priam, Kent Opera, 1984 (photo: Roger de Wolf)

Yvonne Minton as Thea and Josephine Barstow as Denise, Covent Garden, 1970 (photo: Zoë Dominic)

Robert Tear as Dov and Thomas Carey as Mel at Covent Garden in 1970 (photo: Zoë Dominic)

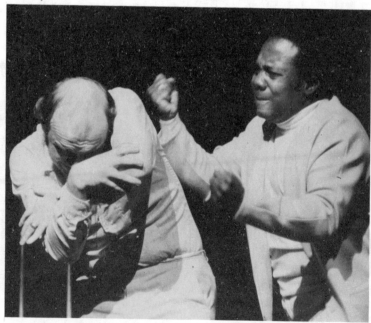

A Tempest of Our Time

Meirion Bowen

The Knot Garden, unlike Tippett's other operas, does not have a conventional, continuous narrative thread. It might better be described, in fact, as fragments from a discourse on love: a series of photographic negatives half revealing the plot that might have been. It lies midway between, say, Puccini-style opera whch is basically mimetic, holding a mirror up to human nature quite explicitly, and another extreme that might be represented by Philip Glass's minimalist operas, freezing everything within a static collection of stylised actions and gestures. *The Knot Garden*, in its own way, offers a set of analytic observations. Each scene presents us with maxims, portraits, states of mind — a metaphorical do-it-yourself kit for the understanding and appreciation of human emotions. This is especially true of Act Three, where the seven characters are involved in charades, sometimes with a division of opinion as to the outcome: *cf.* scene seven —

> Faber-Ferdinand: That scene went wrong! . . .
> . . . Mangus-Prospero: That scene went right!

An opera of this kind could well seem piecemeal. But Tippett ensures that it makes coherent sense. Firstly, the action takes place clearly within the span of a single day. Secondly, the title of the opera provides it with a presiding metaphor: the knot-garden is an allusion to the formalized gardens of French origin, popular in Elizabethan times, normally made of tiny box-hedges and low shrubs, and intended to relate the layout of the garden to the architecture of the house it adjoined; on the other hand, it could be thought of as a maze, or as a rose-garden which 'changes with the inner situations'; in the central act, it is primarily a maze. Thus Tippett offers the producer and designer a firm basis for imaginative, yet tightly-knit, realisations of different kinds.

Moreover, the characters behave consistently throughout the opera as though caught up in a maze. Tippett reinforces this point by introducing associated metaphors. The most important of these comes at the climax of Act Three where the characters reach a state of tentative self-understanding and reconciliation. Tippett here has them sing collectively a couple of lines encapsulating the overall picture of the human condition which his opera has put forward: his lines quote from the world-vision of Goethe's poem, *Das Magische Netz* (*The Magic Net*), which depicts the comings and goings of a group of people dancing with a net:

> We sense the magic net
> That holds us veined
> Each to each to all.

Suddenly everyone is brought together in something approaching harmony. Before that, the personalities in Tippett's opera are encountered mainly in twos and threes rather than singly. Thus, although there is considerable discord within their relationships, it never seems arbitrary or chaotic, nor do the characters appear solipsistically isolated.

The Knot Garden communicates also by virtue of its genre. For Tippett has always had a strong feeling for theatrical tradition: and, distinctive as his operas certainly are, they were never conceived in a vacuum. Thus, opera-goers may here immediately sense a kinship with Mozart's *Così fan tutte*. There is some correspondence between Don Alfonso and Mangus; there are similar pairings-off of characters throughout the action; there is also a streak of irony in both pieces. Theatre-goers, meanwhile, can recognise affinities with Shaw's *Heartbreak House*, with Edward Albee's *Who's Afraid of Virginia Woolf?*, but above all, with Shakespeare's *The Tempest*. Indeed, *The Tempest* provides by far the most obvious reference-point for anyone attending the opera. The libretto of *The Knot Garden* is steeped in allusions to it. Elements in the plot and characterisation are linked: and *The Knot Garden* is (like *Così*) an example of a comedy of forgiveness, of which Shakespeare produced several late examples, *The Tempest* being possibly the best known.

Tippett's operatic figures are perhaps notorious for their habit of suddenly changing gear, moving Jekyll-and-Hyde-like into some alternative dimension of behaviour and utterance. Often, elsewhere in Tippett's *oeuvre*, they revert to historical, mythological or social stereotypes. Here, a strong thread ties such schizoid mannerisms to *The Tempest*. In general, such a method of presenting stage-characters draws attention to their lack of integrity, their vulnerability to traumas, their fondness for dreaming, their potentiality for losing self-control and liability to behave on impulse or to follow animal instincts with often horrific results. It may, highlighted in this way, appear extreme or exaggerated. It is, however, an invitation to the audience to examine its own behaviour. And, indeed, if we analyse a single day in our lives in the Tippett-ian manner, we could well find just as much strangeness, tension and illogicality in our dealings with friends and associates. While *The Knot Garden* eschews actuality of time and place to concentrate upon its psychological probings, it nevertheless bears directly upon life here and now in the second half of the twentieth century.

Tippett's music is, of course, the most vital factor enabling us to identify and experience the plethora of different meanings and symbolic references within the plot and characterisation. This is achieved by the interplay of motifs within a musical mosaic-scheme — perhaps the most sophisticated in all Tippett's music, and certainly one of the most apposite uses of this technique since he crystallised it for the first time in *King Priam*. The music is on the whole fast-moving and, as such, a perfect vehicle for the cinematic mode of presentation which eliminates normal operatic transitions and substitutes so-called 'dissolves' (marked by repeated appearances of purely schematic music — or 'non-music', as the composer was tempted to call it).

At the start of the opera, we have a storm. It corresponds to the magical storm at the start of *The Tempest*, but is more indicative of the psychological storm that is about to burst on us. The storm-motif:

a twelve-note theme, played in octaves by wind and strings, but never consciously thought of as the inception of a dodecaphonically structured work — is present throughout the opera in various transformations. It is at its most tense in the rhythmically contracted versions that introduce the whirling of the characters within the maze at successive points in Act Two. At two points in the opera it is telescoped harmonically to underlie a lyrical expansion of the motif: where Denise and Mel (in Act Two, scene seven) suddenly find common ground, and at the end of Act Three, where Thea and Faber are at last able to communicate with one another. The final scene of reconciliation is signalled by the storm-motif going into reverse.

The three acts of *The Knot Garden* are entitled, in turn, *Confrontation*, *Labyrinth* and *Charade*. The music for each act is distinguishable in relation to these overall dramatic purposes. Act One presents the characters in disarray. Faber's angular vocal lines exhibit his preoccupation with practical everyday concerns (as implied in his name, whose Latin origin signifies a maker or an engineer). Thea, his wife, with whom he cannot communicate, has withdrawn into the privacy of her garden, her inner world of sensuality, as Tippett graphically depicts it in a motif for three horns and strings. These are the two figures who remain almost resolutely opposed until the end of the opera. The confrontations of Act One continue with the innocent cries of their ward, the virginal, adolescent Flora, taunted by the half-imagined, half-real sexual threats of Faber, musically manifest in a jaunty trumpet tune. Here, in fact, is the first of the many brief ritual dances which Tippett uses to show the interplay of characters. It is grotesque and distorted in manner and becomes even more so after Thea has intervened and Faber, left alone, muses on his marital breakdown.

The confrontations now become a fantasy of an overtly Alice-in-Wonderland kind when the musician Dov and his friend Mel, a Negro writer, arrive, interrupting Flora's dreamy humming to herself of a children's counting-song. ('Eeny, meeny, miney moe'). The homosexual relationship between Dov and Mel has broken down. They can only pretend it holds by 'playing a scene together': thus they enact a bizarre ritual dance of their own, expressing their enmity in terms of the playful conflict between Caliban and Ariel. When Thea arrives with a tray of cocktails, she reverts to the mythological archetype enshrined in her name (Circe) and symbolically seduces Mel away into her 'garden', leaving Dov distraught, only able to vent his grief by howling like a dog. Faber, re-entering, finds Dov's behaviour curious: as Dov braves out the situation by pretending simply to be putting on an act, (here Tippett combines the original Mel-Dov dance-tune with musical commentary), and there is a hint of understanding between them: but their potential intimacy is quickly shattered with the return of Thea and Mel and the arrival of Denise, a freedom-fighter (named after the martyr St Denys).

Already in Act One, the interactions between the characters have been set in motion by a psychiatrist, Mangus. He is there at the centre of the storm that opened the opera: and he himself is under the illusion that he is a 'man of power', that he can put things right eventually. He too dreams himself back into a past role, that of Prospero in *The Tempest*. His 'magic' motif (a texture of repeated notes and figurations on flutes, celesta and harp with an undertow of horn, bass-clarinet, and drum notes) is an important ingredient in Tippett's mosaic-scheme (Ex. 2).

The presence of Denise, however, introduces another catalyst into the action. Her long aria, searingly expressive of the suffering she has endured in (presumably) some political cause, serves ultimately to galvanise all the dissarray around her into one lengthy ritual dance — a slow blues, with a fast boogie middle section, enabling everyone to express his or her individual standpoint. This final ensemble of Act One is its climax of dissension and non-communication: even Mangus can only detach himself and (quoting Prospero) doubt his own powers:

> And my ending is despair   Which pierces so, that it assaults
> Unless I be relieved by prayer   Mercy itself, and frees all faults.

This ensemble has its counterpart in the ensemble of reconciliation (quoting Goethe) which is the climax of Act Three.

    The conflicts of Act One are now intensified in the Labyrinth of Act Two, where the characters pair off in a fast-changing sequence, attempting unsuccessfully to 'connect' with each other but only managing to move further away. Denise becomes the one factor in this interplay of personalities likely to bring about some accommodation in their behaviour towards each other. Right at the outset of Act Two, she finds common ground with Thea in their vulnerability towards men. She then exhorts Faber to explore those other aspects of his personality — something corresponding to her own 'secret self' — that might help him move towards a better understanding of himself and Thea. After the playful, stylized charade between Dov and Mel of Act One has been transformed into a wild and agonized song and dance sequence — after, in fact, Faber has unwittingly felt some stirring of passion towards Dov — it is Denise again who finds common ground, this time with Mel, as a representative of an oppressed people. Indeed, one of the most moving episodes in the opera, is the way, in the course of their duet, the civil rights song, 'We shall overcome' seeps into the orchestral texture, and Mel joins in at 'O deep in my heart', singing 'as though the words are forced from him'. This is part of the individuation process which Mel is the first to experience properly in the opera. Although the disarray amongst the other characters continues a while, the opera now changes course. It does so decisively when Dov and Flora are thrown together in the final scene of the act. Dov persuades her to alleviate her grief in song. She responds with Schubert's *Die liebe Farbe* (from *Die schöne Müllerin*) — orchestrated by Tippett — singing the first verse in German and then supplying a vocal obbligato to the second in English. But this, as Dov points out, is inadequate. She needs a song of today, which he will provide: hence Dov's own rapturous aria, recollecting his youth in California yet mingling freely metaphors from European and American culture. For a moment, the labyrinth turns into a 'fabulous rose-garden' (cf. Siegmund and Sieglinde together in the first act of *Die Walküre*). The opera can now journey from innocence to experience (though in Dov's case, this will ultimately be in the form of a song-cycle composed separately from the opera, *Songs for Dov*).

Act Three of *The Knot Garden* sees Mangus deliberately instigating compromise amongst the characters, but not necessarily achieving much beyond a greater sense of self-awareness, for himself as much as the others. The charades which they play, utilising their correspondences to figures in *The Tempest*, are brought to the surface, and enable more considerable development as well as juxtaposition and superimposition of the musical material to come into operation. The various dance-motifs are especially subtly elaborated (at the end of the chess-scene between Faber-Ferdinand and Flora-Miranda, for example, where Flora stands up to Faber for the first time and wins her freedom). But neither Mangus nor Denise is 100 per cent in control. Denise, faced with Mel's homosexuality, is suddenly insecure, and leaves in tears: she is still inadequate with anything but a 'public' notion of human relationships in which duty is all-important. Mel follows her, prompted by Dov, who himself is left alone; only Flora can go to a 'brave new world', and she leaves 'radiant, dancing'. Previously, the violence submerged amongst all these figures was brought out in no uncertain terms. Indeed, they all eventually accuse Mangus:

> And what are you, Mangus?
> Man of power?
> Or dabbler: pimp: voyeur?

Mangus is forced to stop all the charades and declare himself (like Prospero) a fake. The diverse references to *The Tempest* are brought together in a climactic ensemble of reconciliation (where Tippett interweaves into the texture quotations from his own songs for an Old Vic Theatre production of the play in 1961). The message of *The Knot Garden* is bleak:

| If for a timid moment | Exit from the inner cage |
| We submit to love | Turn each to each to all. |

But it is sufficient for Thea and Faber to come to terms with each other and begin their relationship afresh: she 'puts away the seed packets'; he 'puts away the factory papers'. 'The curtain rises' in their lives as it falls in the opera. Their world of actuality emerges from the operatic world of dreams.

Although *The Knot Garden* was commissioned by The Royal Opera House, Covent Garden and first performed there in December, 1970, with Colin Davis conducting, Peter Hall as producer, Timothy O'Brien as designer and costumes by Tazeena Firth, it perhaps belongs more intrinsically to smaller theatres. Its US première took place in just such a venue, the Cahn Auditorium at Northwestern University, Evanston, Illinois in February 1974, with a student cast conducted by Bernard Rubenstein. Yet there seemed to be a disparity between the large orchestra (inlcuding piano, electric guitar, and much percussion) which it entailed and the intimate stage-action involving only seven characters and no chorus. Moreover, this disparity was more apparent than real, since the sound of the scoring was never at odds with the stage action.

In fact, when in 1982, at the request of the Opera Factory I investigated the possibility of reducing the orchestra of *The Knot Garden* to chamber-ensemble proportions, so that it could be presented in small theatres, I discovered that there was no real problem. For so much soloistic writing existed in the piece that, in general, it was illusory to think of it as having a full orchestral accompaniment at all. The string textures were such that they could be undertaken by solo players, as long as some balance problems were resolved.

Thus, when the newly formed Opera Factory London Sinfonietta decided to mount several performances of the opera in 1984, and the composer agreed that a chamber version was desirable, I planned it so that the minimum number of players required would be 22. Not a note of Tippett's music was changed in this reduction. About a third of each act required instrumental re-deployment (rather than re-orchestration); and in the rest, a certain amount of doctoring facilitated the 'faking' of sonorities such as those of two piccolos or two double-basses. Many pages of the score required no adjustments whatsoever (or only minor ones). For balance purposes I omitted a xylophone and occasionally reinforced *tutti* passages. In rationalising the percussion parts so that only two players were needed, I sometimes asked other players in the ensemble to perform on percussion when they were unused for several pages on end. The chamber version requires versatility but no more virtuosity than was demanded by the original. It need not supplant the original, but simply make it more economic to put the opera on in small theatres.

The best compliment paid about the revised version was that listeners could not distinguish it from the original. Nonetheless, there were some criticisms, specifically about the strength of sonority in the very opening of Act One; also the lack of a rich string orchestra sound in the duet for Denise and Mel in Act Two. I have now tried to reinforce these passages, discreetly; but it may not be possible to produce an ideal solution to the second episode in question without, perhaps, using a string synthesiser: rather, I am inclined to feel that this will become accepted in the context of the chamber version as it is more widely heard and the original is not insistently at the back of listeners' minds. Meanwhile, having a revised version of *The Knot Garden* available will enable it to be more widely produced: which is something it deserves, since (in my view) it has the most consistent marriage of words, music and dramatic action of all the Tippett operas.

The Knot Garden

An Opera in Three Acts by Michael Tippett

Libretto by Michael Tippett

Dedicated to Sir David Webster
of The Royal Opera House, Covent Garden

The Knot Garden was first performed at The Royal Opera House, Covent Garden on December 2, 1970. The first performance in the United States was at the North Western University Opera Theater in Evanston, Illinois on February 22, 1974.

*'The play within a play': Robert Tear as Dov/Ariel, Raimund Herincx as Faber/
Ferdinand, Thomas Hemsley as Mangus/Prospero, Josephine Barstow as Denise, Yvonne
Minton as Thea, Jill Gomez as Flora/Miranda and Thomas Carey as Mel/Caliban;
Covent Garden, 1970 (photo: Stuart Robinson)*

CHARACTERS

Faber *a civil engineer, aged about 35* — *robust baritone*
Thea *his wife, a gardener* — *dramatic mezzo*
Flora *their ward, an adolescent girl* — *light high soprano*
Denise *Thea's sister, a dedicated freedom-fighter* — *dramatic soprano*
Mel *a negro writer in his late twenties* — *lyric bass baritone*
Dov *his white friend, a musician* — *lyric tenor*
Mangus *an analyst* — *high tenor baritone*

The scene, whether labyrinth or rosegarden, changes with the inner situations. If the garden were ever finally visible, it might be a high-walled house-garden shutting out an industrial city. The labyrinth, on the other hand, can never be actual. It appears, if at all, as a maze which continually shifts and possibly (in Act Two) spins.

Time is the present. Although the duration is obviously within one day, from getting up to bedtime, the dramatic action is discontinuous, more like the cutting of a film. The term used for these cuts is 'Dissolve', implying some deliberate break-up and re-formation of the stage picture.

Thomas Hemsley as Mangus and Yvonne Minton as Thea, Covent Garden, 1970 (photo: Zoë Dominic)

'. . .simply the thing I am shall make me live.'

Act One

Confrontation

Scene One. *Mangus appears to be lying on a couch as a still point in a whirling storm. When the storm subsides he rises from the couch and looks out over the audience.* [1]

MANGUS

So, if I dream,
It's clear I'm Prospero:
Man of power.
He put them all to rights. [2]

At a gesture from him the couch disappears. He holds for a moment a pose of self-satisfaction.

Dissolve.

Scene Two. *Thea is coming slowly from the inner garden, stooping occasionally to tend the flowers. She reaches Mangus.*

THEA

What did you want, Mangus?

MANGUS
(turning)

Ah, Thea.
I thought I'd help you in your garden.

With a conjuror's flourish he produces a pair of secateurs.

I could cut the roses.

THEA
(with authority)

Only I may prune this garden.
Give me the secateurs.
Planting is rough;
Yet needs green, loving fingers.
(taking the secateurs)
Pruning is the crown.
Mangus, your finesse lies elsewhere.
Mine lies in my garden,
(turning away)
Where I touch the tap-root
To my inward sap.

They hold a meditative pose for a moment.

Scene Three. *Off stage screams; then Flora rushes on. She hesitates for a second as if instantaneously assessing the two immobile figures, before she flings herself into Thea's arms.*

FLORA
(whimpering)

Ah — ee, ah — ee.

Faber enters. Flora has a fit of trembling and buries herself deeper into Thea.

THEA

Come, Flora, stop crying.
Go with Mangus.

Mangus takes Flora away towards the inner garden.

Scene Four.

THEA
(turning upon Faber)

What is it you do to Flora?
What is it you want?
Faber, I demand
You look into yourself;
Cut the offensive action
Out once and for all.
Flora's a seedling
Waiting to transplant;
Bud not-flower.
If I may mother her: not over much,
You should father her,
Not play the lecher.

She follows Flora and Mangus into the inner garden.

Scene Five.

FABER

A mother bitch!
Who turns me to a cur.
A mother bitch!
And yet my wife.
O Thea,
How did we fall today
Out of the mutual bed
Apart?
Today! Each day.
The usual! Habitual!
Till Thea withdraws into her garden.
(half to himself, half to Mangus who has returned)
I do not flirt with Flora.
Flora screams before I . . .

Further thought is too painful. He looks at his watch.

Impossible!
(assuming an habitual pose; directly to Mangus)
Please tell my wife I've gone to work.

He goes out.

Scene Six.

MANGUS

World without; world within:
Withdrawal to the factory or the garden.
Wherever the partner cannot follow!
'Please tell my wife . . .'
The usual, habitual
Words that mask emotions till . . .
Till what?
Till life explodes.
Or till the priest-magician . . .
What's the quote?
    (*as Prospero to his daughter*)
Attend Miranda!
    (*quoting with exaggerated rhetoric*)
'And by my prescience
I find my zenith doth depend upon
A most auspicious star.'
But who, I ask,
Who sets the star in such an aspect?
All accident: fortuitous: begin here.

    Mangus disappears.

    Dissolve.

Scene Seven.

THEA

You can pick roses,
Arrange them in a bowl.

FLORA
    (*humming*)

Mn, mn, mn, mn.

THEA

Flora! You're day-dreaming.

FLORA

I'm sorry.
Oh, and I forgot.
A message from Denise. Your sister?
She comes here, today, later.

THEA

So she is home, Denise, my sister.
The turbulent girl grown to a woman.

    Thea goes off.

Scene Eight. *Flora is pleased to be alone.
She wanders around humming to herself.
Eventually she appears to be choosing be-
tween some of the garden flowers.*

FLORA

Eeny, meeny, miney, mo.
Catch a nigger by his toe.
If he hollers . . .

Scene Nine. *She jumps up as she is
interrupted suddenly by a hullabaloo as Dov
and Mel enter. They are in fancy dress. Dov
as Ariel; Mel as Caliban. That is, Mel is fish-
like (as was Caliban) and 'swims' on, with*

*Dov (Ariel in 'The Tempest' takes once the
guise of a water-nymph) trying to hook him.
They come to rest and remain so immobile
that Flora comes gingerly forward as if to
touch them.*

DOV

(*suddenly; spoken with exaggeratedly broad
vowels like an English stage caricature of a
North American*)

'If you think we're waxworks, you ought to
pay, you know. Waxworks weren't made to
be looked at for nothing. No how!'

MEL

(*spoken in a preternaturally low voice like a
stage caricature of the Deep South*)

'Contrariwise, if you think we're alive, you
ought to speak.'

FLORA

(*involuntarily; spoken with a tiny voice like
a stage Alice*)

'I'm sure I'm very sorry.'
(*passionately with a slight tremor in her
voice*)
Oh, do stop play-acting;
I'm real somewhere; I'm Flora.

DOV AND MEL
    (*breaking the pose*)

We're real too, somewhere.

*They look to each other for agreement, then
nod.*

MEL

I'm Mel. I write . . . words.

DOV

Contrariwise, I'm Dov. I write . . . music.

MEL

But because we're . . .

DOV

. . . acting . . .

MEL

. . . a scene together, for . . .

DOV

. . . the moment . . .

MEL

. . . he's Ariel.

DOV

Contrariwise, he's Caliban.

They laugh and start to dance round Flora.

DOV AND MEL

Ca — ca — Caliban
Was a bad man
But Ariel was fairy.
He could fly through the air

Invisible
But Caliban was scaly.

As the ditty finishes Thea and Mangus come from the house. Thea has a tray of cocktails.

Scene Ten.
THEA
(*after an icy silence*)

Children at play.

She goes to put the tray on the table.

MANGUS

Adults too play later:
Plays within the play.
Ariel, Caliban, Ferdinand, Miranda:
All shall appear when I play Prospero.
Flora, come with me.
We need more costumes.

They go off together. The triangle-trio that is left survey each other as in a ritual dance. Each man takes a glass from Thea's tray and she takes one herself. They lift the glasses to drink. As they do so Mel is drawn away to Thea so that Dov is isolated. Thea like Circe draws Mel hypnotically, by implication sexually, into the garden. Dov smashes his glass to smithereens.

Scene Eleven.
DOV
(*on all fours, howling, like Ariel's dog*)

Bow — wow, Bow — wow.
Ow, ow, ow.

Scene Twelve. *He is still in this state when Faber returns. Faber looks at the apparition in astonishment. Dov, to brave it out, repeats the song.*

DOV

Ca — ca — Caliban
Was a bad man
But Ariel was fairy.
He could fly through the air
Invisible
But Caliban was scaly.

FABER

Who in hell are you?

DOV

My name is Dov; a musician.
For the moment, as you see,
I'm dressed as Ariel.

FABER

'But Ariel was fairy'
Who then is Caliban?

DOV

My friend Mel is Caliban.
(Or will be when we play the scene.)

FABER

A curious friend.

DOV

We share together.
(Or did till now.)

FABER

I see. I see.
Come closer: to me: Faber.

By implication sexually provocative, Faber whistles jauntily. Dov moves across the stage as though fascinated. But before they meet, and with a strange sobbing cry from the orchestra, Thea and Mel are there on the opposite side of the stage. The resultant tableau cannot become a vocal ensemble because the tensions are not ready for such expression. As soon therefore as we have had time enough to appreciate the emotions each might be feeling, Flora runs on and the potentialities for development into a scene are exploded.

Scene 13. / Finale
FLORA

Ah-ee, ah-ee.
Thea, Thea,
Denise is come . . .
She looks, she looks . . .
Oh, I can't tell you . . .

MANGUS
(*entering behind Flora and half engulfed in the masses of coloured costumes he carries; looking out over the audience*)

We be but men of sin.
So sounds the accusation.

He sets down the costumes in a heap, by the table of cocktails. Denise enters half-majestic, half-sinister. She is twisted or otherwise disfigured from the effects of torture. After each few steps lights flash like lightning and during each flash the other characters take their places step by step for the aria to come. It is possible also that in order for the heap of costumes and the table to be properly counterpointed visually against Denise, they will have grown much larger. When the operation is complete Denise entirely dominates the stage.

DENISE

Oh, you may stare in horror.
I was straight before they twisted me.
Ah, ah.
Angels have fought angels
As man has fought man
If the command comes
To redeem our manhood
From a bestial time.
Ah, ah.
When we were tortured
We screamed.

103

Ah, ah.
Indecent anguish of the quivering flesh.
Ah, ah.
Until we broke.
Or they stopped.
Ah, ah.
I want no pity.
This distortion is my pride.
I want no medal.
The lust of violence has bred
Contamination in my blood.
I cannot forget.
I will not forgive.
Ah, ah.
How can I turn home again to you,
The beautiful and damned?

As there is no immediate answer to her question, Denise remains aloof. Only Mel reaches for some kind of alleviation by going over into a discharge of emotion in the blues.

MEL
(in the style and accent of a negro bluesman)

Do, do not, do not torment me,
Baby, do not torment me,
'cause I'm a no-good man.

DOV
(imitating Mel's style and accent)

Do, do not, do not desert me,
Brother, do not desert me,
'cause I'm a two-way man.

FLORA
(imitating Mel's style and accent)

Do, do not, do not assault me,
Please, do not assault me,
Lover, don't you see,
I'm a little girl lost.

FABER
(imitating Mel's style and accent)

You'd like to take the mickey out of me,
Woman, you'd like to take the mickey out of me.
'cause I'm gonna play the high-class joints,
I'm gonna play the low-class joints,
And, baby, I'm even gonna play the honky-tonks.
You'd like to take the mickey out of me?

THEA
(in her own style)

Can this play-boy be my true man?
Lord, can this play-boy be my man?
Shall he father my children?
Will he shelter my home?
(imitating Mel's style and accent)
'Well, I walk, talk — but all by myself.
I walk, talk — but all by myself.'
(in her own style)
Alone in my garden.

MEL
Do I have a witness out there?

FLORA AND DOV
(answering Mel)

All right, brother.

MEL
Do I have a witness out there?

FLORA AND DOV
All right, brother.

MEL, FLORA AND DOV
Go, tell it from the mountain,
Tell it like it is.

MEL
So I sing the blues for me, baby.
Maybe sing the blues for you?
The black man sing the blues for Mr
    Charlie?

DOV
So you take it where you find it, brother,
Or leave it like it is.
That's the way it's always been,
That's the way love is.

FLORA
So I don't know who I am, lover,
Don't know who I'll be,
All I know right now, honey,
's that I'm a little girl lost.

FABER
Come on baby, come on please,
Come on baby, baby, please,
Turn on the light, let it shine on me,
Turn on your love light, let it shine on me.

THEA
(in her own style)

Can this play-boy be my true man?
Lord, can this play-boy be my man?
Will he never come with me
Deep into my garden?

DENISE
(high above everyone)

Ah, ah.

MANGUS
(to the audience, as Prospero)

And my ending is despair
Unless I be relieved by prayer
Which pierces so, that it assaults
Mercy itself, and frees all faults.

MEL
Sure, baby.

Curtain.

Act Two

Labyrinth

Here the garden is in total disarray and the maze in operation. That is, it appears as if the centre of the stage had the power to 'suck in' a character at the back of the stage, say, and 'eject' him at the front. During their passage through the maze, characters meet and play out their scenes. But always one of the characters in these scenes is about to be ejected, while a fresh character has been sucked in and is whirled to the meeting point. Indeed, if the maze could be seen from above, it might be apparent that someone, perhaps Mangus, is operating a huge puppet show. And this means that when two characters play a scene the one or the other may be whisked away arbitrarily, independent of where the scene has got to, as by force majeure. Finally the two characters most lost and most alone are thrown clear of the maze onto the forestage, and the maze recedes from attention.

Scene One. *Thea and Denise, the sisters, are the first to be whirled to the meeting point. But although they are fully aware of each other, they do not properly converse. They act as in a dream or nightmare. At the arbitrary moment, Thea is 'ejected' and Faber is whirled into position.*

THEA

Fear!
What do I fear?
Do I fear for?
Not the inner garden;
Ah no:
My home.
Where the bond to Faber in the mutual bed
Renders me
Vulnerable.
And to my sister?
Love?
Jealousy!
Candour: my sole strength.
Denise, Denise . . .

DENISE

Fear!
What do I fear?
Do I fear for?
Not the core of freedom;
Ah no:
My goal.
Risking a woman's bond in love now
Renders me
Vulnerable.

And to my sister?
Love?
Envy!

She tries to reach Denise but is whirled off around the back as Faber is whirled on.

Scene Two. *Scene Two, though more naturalistic than Scene One, is played as if by puppets, especially Faber.*

FABER

Thea shuns me.
You do not.

DENISE

Thea no doubt has reasons.
I have none.

FABER

Thea sulks in her garden
When I most need her.
Or do I need her?
Or her alone?

DENISE

I do not know your needs:
I hardly know my own.

FABER

'I hardly know my own.'
There sounds a mutual echo.
Let us explore.

DENISE

You are deceived.
I have a secret self
As tough as Thea's;
As you should have — may have, for all I know.
There's nothing to explore.
I have no need of you.

Denise is whirled away and Flora is whirled on. She is quite lost, still trying to choose between her flowers.

Scene Three.

FLORA

Eeny, meeny, miney, mo.
   (*continually backing away from Faber*)
Ah — ee, ah — ee.

FABER

This is absurd.
Flora, come here.

105

What are you afraid of?
Grow up: grow up.
You're not a girl now, you're a woman.
Do you hear?
Give me those flowers.
Stand I tell you.

*But Flora, who has only responded to
Faber's attack with tiny whimpers of sound,
drops the flowers and, terrified, is mercifully
whirled off as Thea is again whirled on.*

Scene Four.

THEA
(*striking Faber with a horse-whip*)

Take that; take that;
You cur, you coward;
As all men are
Beneath their arrogance.
Without the divine Furies,
Who are women,
There'd be no retribution:
Cleansing, correcting.
Take that, take that.

*Faber defends himself from the whip-lashes
as best he can, but is forced to the ground, on
all fours. Thea. is whirled off and Dov,
dressed now as himself, is whirled on.*

Scene Five.

DOV
(*ironic*)

Bow — wow, Bow — wow.
Ow, ow, ow.
Has some woman put you down?

FABER

Ah! Dov: you should know.
Has a woman never put you down?

DOV

No: no woman.
Not directly:
At second-hand.

FABER
(*ironic*)

But those howls —
Ow, ow, ow —
Were cries of love, I take it,
Not of hate?

DOV

Self-pity (more likely)
Or heartbreak.

FABER

Heartbreak: good grief!
And dare I guess
The cause, the agent;
That man of honey:
Mel?

DOV

Not honey: bitter.
Or bitter-sweet;
Like music.
What are you at, Faber?
Probing to mock?

FABER

I'm curious.
I had to know
You — Dov, what if I
Want you: have power
To tempt, to force? Come,
I never kissed a man before.

*But he is whirled away while Mel, dressed
now as himself, is whirled on.*

Scene Six. *Mel and Dov play this scene like
a song and dance number against a fast and
bitter blues background.*

MEL

You love the manhood
Not the man
You make your god.
Strip off the sham!

DOV

I love you.

TOGETHER

One day we meet together, brother,
One day we meet together, brother,
One day we move apart.

MEL

You call me brother where's no family
Between black and white.
Strip off the sham!

DOV

The heart's my family.

TOGETHER

One day we meet together, brother,
One day we meet together, brother,
One day we move apart.

DOV

Who's to be despised, myself or the fake
Who came so close?
Admit the shame!

MEL

No shame. I loved you, but
One day we meet together, brother,
One day we meet together, brother,
One day we move apart.

DOV

Bow — wow
Bow — wow
Ow, ow, ow, ow.

106

MEL

Stop howling now.
Become yourself:
Go turn your howls to music.

Dov is whirled away as Denise is whirled on.

Scene Seven. *Denise addresses Mel, who comments as though to himself.*

DENISE

Music is bitter-sweet:
Words are weapons
In the fight
For freedom, justice, dignity.
Your race calls you,
Calls for your words,
For your strength, for your love.
And I,
Who fight for all true causes,
Should I not follow such a man?

MEL

So let Dov go.
A man is for real.
A man is for real.
(*As though hearing in his mind 'We Shall Overcome', words are forced from him:*)
'Oh, deep in my heart . . .'
So let Denise enter.
Now turn about.

Scene Eight. *As Mel turns to Denise, the maze appears suddenly to go into reverse and is violently accelerated. Dov returns first.*

DOV
(*mocking*)

. . . where's no family
Between black and white!

If Mel doesn't actually throw him, Dov is certainly ejected prone onto the forestage. Thea returns.

MEL
(*to Thea, mocking*)

Go water your roses!

He is whirled away after Denise.

THEA
(*alone*)

Briars and thorns!

Flora returns, running from Faber. She avoids Thea's protecting arms, and in so doing is thrown clear onto the forestage, prone and sobbing. Thea and Faber face each other for a moment.

Dissolve.

Scene Nine. *As the sense of nightmare clears away, Dov comes to life first. He sees the plight of Flora and goes to comfort her.*

DOV
(*kneeling at her side*)

Flora: Flora, love;
Stop crying.
There's only you and me.

Flora gradually recovers composure.

FLORA

I'm glad it's you.

He rocks her gently in his arms.

DOV

Flora, do you like music?
(Music that's bitter-sweet.)
Do you ever sing?

FLORA
(*sitting up on her own*)

'In grün will ich mich kleiden,
In grüne Tränenweiden:
Mein Schatz hat's grün so gern.'

DOV
(*translating musingly*)

'I will dress myself in green,
In green weeping-willows:
My love's so fond of green':
But that's a boy's song.

FLORA

Sometimes I dream I am a boy,
Who dies for love.
And then I am a girl again.
Dov, you understand.

DOV

Yes, I understand.
Yet you're a bud that hasn't opened.
Let's sing a different song.

He stands up to sing his first song.

I was born in a big town,
In a home without a garden.
I was born in a big town
Where the buildings grew so mighty high
(O boy!), high enough to scrape the sky.
Play it cool, play it cool.

Come with me to the warm south
Or the golden Californian west.
Come with me to the warm south
Where the palm trees grow so mighty tall
(O boy!), tall enough to shade us all.
Play it cool, play it cool.

Oh hold our fleeting youth for ever.
Oh stop the world I want to get off.
Oh honey, honey, make love to me
Now (Oh boy!), now (how play it cool?)
In the fabulous rose-garden.

Under the influence of Dov's music the rose-garden begins to form. By the last verse of the song it is all there: the enclosing walls, the fountain, the girl, the lover, the music. As the song ends, a shadow enters the garden. It is Mel. He taps the lovers on the shoulders.

MEL

Come: I taught you that.

DOV
(*leaping up*)

It is false.

The garden fades. The young people look on in dismay.

Curtain.

The 1984 Opera Factory London Sinfonietta production by David Freeman, sets by David Roger and costumes by Belinda Scarlett. Nigel Robson as Dov/Ariel trapped in the cloven pine and Omar Ebrahim as Mel/Caliban (photo: Malcolm Crowthers)

Act Three

Charade

Five of the characters in the opera have roles in the Charade: Mangus-Prospero, Dov-Ariel, Mel-Caliban, Flora-Miranda, Faber-Ferdinand. These roles are never absolute; they are dropped at need. Thea and Denise remain themselves. Anyone may be a spectator when not playing a scene in the Charade.

Scene One.

MANGUS
(putting on his cloak)

You must both hold with me.
Not for ever, but for now.
The play has bewildering moments.
(circling his wand)
Imagine those walls are rocks,
The howling sea beyond,
This garden now an island.

THEA
(ironic)

Where you play Prospero,
Man of power;
To set the world to rights!

MANGUS

The power is in the play.

DENISE
(stepping into Mangus's circle)

Power is in the will.

THEA
(stepping into Mangus's circle; crying out)

Forgiveness.
Blood from my breast.
Here on this island
I know no god but love.

Dissolve.

Scene Two. *Mangus-Prospero and Flora-Miranda are exploring the island on their first day. Miranda is as old as in 'The Tempest'. Mel-Caliban is crawling about, dumb.*

MEL-CALIBAN
(grunting)

Ugh — ugh — ugh — ugh.

FLORA-MIRANDA

Whatever's that?

MANGUS-PROSPERO

Even desert islands have a history.

(consulting his book)
According to my book that beast is Caliban,
Orphaned moronic offspring to the foul
   witch, Sycorax.

MEL-CALIBAN

Ugh — ugh — ugh — ugh.

FLORA-MIRANDA

And must we live with him?

MANGUS-PROSPERO

I fear so.
Yet I have art to tame him;
To civilize: yes, that's the word.
(using his wand as a trainer's stick)
Come up now: come up now.

Mel-Caliban tries to stand upright.

FLORA-MIRANDA
(clapping her hands)

How clever you are, father!

Cries come from a nearby tree.

DOV-ARIEL
(in the tree; shouted at high pitch)

Free — ee — dom. Free — ee — dom.
Ai — ir — r. Li — gh — ght.

FLORA-MIRANDA

And that?

MANGUS-PROSPERO

He's been there for centuries,
Ariel: spirit of the air,
Feckless, unconstrained.
He angered Sycorax who shut him in the
   tree.
So when she died, none could let him out.

DOV-ARIEL

Free — ee — dom. Free — ee — dom.
Ai — ir — r. Li — gh — ght.

MANGUS-PROSPERO

Hold the book open at the proper page,
And I'll undo him.

FLORA-MIRANDA

How kind you are, father!

MANGUS-PROSPERO

Caliban and Ariel:
Mine to command;
Theirs to be grateful.

Using the wand he splits open the tree. With a whoop Dov-Ariel rushes out and flings himself on Mel-Caliban who is knocked off his precarious balance.

DOV-ARIEL

Your filthy mother, Sycorax, is dead;
But you're alive alright.
I've waited centuries for this.

He belabours Mel-Caliban.

FLORA-MIRANDA

O father, help, help!

MANGUS-PROSPERO
(hauling Dov-Ariel off)

Stop, stop: what's this?

DOV-ARIEL

Hands off: I do but play my part.

MEL-CALIBAN

Oh no: you go beyond the script.

DOV-ARIEL

As I shall always do.

MANGUS-PROSPERO

Control yourselves: obey!

FLORA-MIRANDA

Here, father, your book.

Dissolve.

Scene Three.

THEA

Two unruly spirits born!
Ah, Prospero,
Scenes turn in the hand,
Beyond your book,
When played by persons.

DENISE

I do not understand confusion.
Before an assignment
The mood was dedication and the mind was
    clear:
To kill, even, or be killed.
Extreme: accurate: cold.

THEA

Mel will warm you, sister.

DENISE

Mel will uphold me as I am.

THEA

In love the purities are mixed.

DENISE

Never.

Dissolve.

Scene Four. *Flora-Miranda is asleep. Dov-Ariel is on guard. Mangus-Prospero is watching through a telescope. Mel-Caliban creeps on and up to the sleeping girl. Mangus-Prospero signals to Dov-Ariel to be ready. Mel-Caliban suddenly leaps on Flora-Miranda; pinning her arms, he tries to tear the clothes off her. She wakes and screams. At the dramatic instant Denise appears and hauls Mel-Caliban off and to his feet. Flora-Miranda runs off.*

Scene Five.

DENISE

Mel! Oh, crude: oh, obscene:
Oh, distorted from your truth.

MEL-CALIBAN

I play the role he gives me.
No more.

DENISE

No more?
Oh yes, there's more.

MEL

What?
That I'm a sensual man?
Come, lay your head against my pounding
    heart.

DOV

Where my head often lay.

DENISE

Oh, I am torn: tortured
By shocks I had not known.
Ah, ah. Ah, ah.
I break.

She goes away in tears.

DOV

Go, man, follow.
Go, man, follow.
For what am I
But shadow puppet on another's screen?

MEL

I follow; I follow.
I follow; I follow.
Though what am I
But black earth for the white roses?

Mel goes.

THEA
(acidly)

And what are you, Mangus?
Man of power?
Or dabbler: pimp: voyeur?

MANGUS-PROSPERO
(with dignity, handing the telescope to Thea)

Take the glass yourself.
Now by my art

You shall savour such a scene
Of tender reconciliation
As dreams may show,
Holding the mirror up to nature.
Ariel: disclose.

Scene Six. *Dov-Ariel discloses Faber-Ferdinand and Flora-Miranda playing chess. Faber-Ferdinand turns his head to be visible to the audience.*

THEA

Ah no!

MANGUS-PROSPERO

Be still.

FLORA-MIRANDA
(*quoting with exaggerated rhetoric: a caricature of false innocence*)

'Sweet Lord, you play me false!'

FABER-FERDINAND
(*quoting with exaggerated rhetoric: a caricature of false charm*)

'No my dearest love,
I would not for the world.'

FLORA-MIRANDA
(*sending the chess-board flying*)

Oh, yes you would.
False, false.
Dov-Ariel, lend me your wings.
I'm free: I'm free.

She runs off. Dov-Ariel follows.

Scene Seven.

FABER-FERDINAND

That scene went wrong!

THEA

Ah!

MANGUS-PROSPERO

That scene went right!

THEA

Ah!

MANGUS-PROSPERO
(*to Faber-Ferdinand*)

Collect the pieces: repair the board.
(*turning to Thea*)
Collect: collect.

FABER-FERDINAND
(*on his knees, searching*)

Here's the king.

MANGUS-PROSPERO

Then set him up.

THEA
(*rising from her knees*)

And here's the queen.
Catch.

She throws the piece to Faber-Ferdinand and a burst of bright music greets the action.

MANGUS-PROSPERO

Not so fast.
There are pawns missing.
(*to Faber-Ferdinand*)
Come.

They disappear.

THEA
(*alone*)

I am no more afraid.
So we swing full-circle back
Towards the sanctuary of marriage.
O strange enigma!
This morning my garden seemed a
sanctuary
From where I hated him and fought all day.
Now, now, I know
Nature is us.
O strange enigma!
I am no more afraid.

She goes.

Dissolve.

Scene Eight.

FLORA-MIRANDA
(*dancing around gaily*)

Goodbye island: goodbye cave.
Goodbye sweet Ariel: ugly Caliban.

She stops.

But what of them, father?
Are they left behind?

MANGUS-PROSPERO

That troubles me.
They demand quittance and release.
Assuming all power, now
I must play the offensive role.
Nerves: be steel.

Mangus-Prospero takes position as a kind of judge; Faber-Ferdinand is some sort of jailor. Dov-Ariel is brought on in handcuffs.

FABER-FERDINAND
(*in a flat speaking voice and with an appropriate dialect accent*)

He's gone off his food.
His wings are drooping.
He used to sing before.

MANGUS-PROSPERO
(*quoting with exaggerated rhetoric*)

'How now? moody?
What is't thou canst demand?'

111

DOV-ARIEL
(quoting with exaggerated rhetoric)

'My liberty.'

MANGUS-PROSPERO

He always was the skilled servant,
And there's no power without agents.
Yet I've no power more to hold him.
Set him free!

Faber-Ferdinand strikes the handcuffs from the prisoner.

DOV-ARIEL
(dancing)

Fettered: now free.
Music my muse.

FLORA-MIRANDA

That was fine, father.

Mel-Caliban is brought on in handcuffs.

FABER-FERDINAND
(in a flat speaking voice and with an appropriate dialect accent)

He sings alright;
A pulsing, violent, sexy song.
        (quoting with exaggerated rhetoric)
'But he's a devil, a born devil.'
            (in the flat speaking voice)
You're better without him.

MANGUS-PROSPERO

Oh no — 'he doth make our fire,
Fetch our wood, and serves in offices
That profit us: what hoa: slave: Caliban:
Thou earth, thou: speak.'

MEL-CALIBAN
(quoting with exaggerated rhetoric)

'This island's mine, by Sycorax my mother.
And I am all the subjects which you have,
Which first was mine own King.'

MANGUS-PROSPERO

King is too much.
You would usurp my place?
Inferior!
Back to the penitentiary or the school.

FLORA-MIRANDA
(crying out)

Father, for pity's sake!
All, all are free.

DOV-ARIEL
(dancing around Mel-Caliban provocatively to taunt him)

Ca — ca — Caliban
            (wolf-whistling)
(Whew, whew)
Was a bad man
(Whew, whew)

And never forget it,
Sang Ariel, for
I'm the king of the castle,
I'm the king of the . . .

With an imperious gesture Mangus-Prospero dismisses the Charade and strides to the footlights.

Scene Nine. / Finale

MANGUS
(speaking direct to the audience)

Enough! Enough!
We look in the abyss.
Lust for Caliban will not save us.
Prospero's a fake, we all know that;
And perhaps the island's due to sink into
    the sea.
Now that I break my staff and drown my
    book . . .

DOV, MEL, FABER

'Full fathom five, thy father lies.'

VOICES OFFSTAGE
(spoken)

'Ding-dong, Ding-dong.'

MANGUS
(spoken)

. . . I'm but a foolish, fond old man,
Just like the rest of you,
Whistling to keep my pecker up . . .

Voices offstage: whistles and bow-wows.

MANGUS
(spoken)

. . . Whistling to a music
Compounded of our groans and shrieks,
Bitter-sweet and wry,
Tender, yet tough: ironic
Celebration for that trickster Eros —

DOV, MEL, FABER

O boy!

MANGUS
(spoken)

— in his masks of love.

All take position for the ensuing ensemble, except Faber and Thea.

ALL

If, for a timid moment
We submit to love,
Exit from the inner cage,
Turn each to each to all
'Come unto these yellow sands' —

VOICES OFF STAGE

'Come, come' —

ALL

Within this theatre, upon this stage,
Here, now, beyond the end-game —

ONE AFTER THE OTHER

Here, here, here, here, here —

ALL

We sense the magic net
That holds us veined
Each to each to all
'Come unto these yellow sands.'

VOICES OFFSTAGE

'Come, come' —

ALL

Hold for a moment, then —

ONE AFTER THE OTHER

Goodbye, goodbye, goodbye, goodbye,
goodbye.

ALL

Bye, bye, bye, bye, bye ...

MANGUS

'Leave not a wrack behind.'

VOICES OFFSTAGE

'No wrack behind.'

The ensemble issues in departure. Mel goes first with Denise. Flora departs alone, radiant, dancing. Though Dov might wish to follow Flora, he cannot. A look back from Mel draws him to follow Mel and Denise.

MANGUS

Look! Look!
Mel going with Denise.
And Flora to her 'brave new world'.
Ah, Dov, I pity you.
Only the two remain.

Mangus disappears.

Dissolve.

Scene Ten. */Epilogue. Thea and Faber are alone in the garden. Thea is perhaps sorting seeds, Faber studying his papers. Or these things are just implied. The vast night gives a huge dimension to the dark around them. After a while they begin to sing, though not to each other.*

THEA

I put away the seed packets.

FABER

I put away the factory papers.

BOTH

I encompass the vast night with an image of
desire.

FABER

Now I stand up: Faber: man: maker:
myself.

THEA

Now I stand up: Thea: woman: mother:
myself.

BOTH

Our enmity's transcended in desire.

THEA

Memory recedes in the moment.

FABER

I am all imagination.

They are about to move to each other.

BOTH

The curtain rises.

Curtain.

'The Ice Break' at Covent Garden, (producer Sam Wanamaker, designer Ralph Koltai, lighting David Hersey, choreography Walter Raines), the 1977 world première: the Paradise Garden; 1979, Lev (John Shirley-Quirk) outside the operating theatre (photos: Zoë Dominic)

Stereotypes and Rebirth

Leslie East

Tippett's fourth (and, he himself maintains, his final) opera was commissioned by The Royal Opera House, Covent Garden and given its world première by The Royal Opera on July 7, 1977. The first production was distinguished by a vivid stage realisation by the American actor-producer, Sam Wanamaker (who cut his operatic teeth on the première of *King Priam*) and typically challenging settings by Ralph Koltai. Sir Colin Davis, the work's dedicatee, directed a cast that mixed familiar Tippett interpreters (Heather Harper, John Shirley-Quirk, Josephine Barstow) with newcomers (the American mezzo Beverly Vaughn, as Hannah, making an outstanding impression) and drew strongly committed contributions from the Covent Garden chorus and orchestra.

Before the revival of this production in 1979, two other companies had taken up the work. A Kiel Festival production in 1978 was plainly influenced by the Covent Garden original but Sarah Caldwell's flawed but ingenious staging in Boston in May 1979 provided a fresh and (within the terms of Tippett's deliberately vague stipulations) perfectly acceptable interpretation (the first professional production of any Tippett opera in the USA).

The Character of the Opera

The Ice Break is an opera of comparative brevity — each act lasts less than half an hour — but it is remarkable for the great compression and speed of its action. The mosaic techniques of *King Priam* and the cinematic processes of *The Knot Garden* are here taken to their extreme, the first act in particular rushing by at a breathtaking tempo.

It is important for the listener to realise straightaway that a conventional approach to this opera will misconstrue its medium and miss its message. Tippett's confessed addiction to TV and film has produced an operatic structure that retains the outlines of conventional arias, duets and ensembles but compresses or even dispenses with transitions so that a cinematic sense of simultaneity is achieved. Scenes end abruptly or apparently overlap. Only in Act Three is there some relaxation of this technique and this has dramatic purpose.

It is also important to accept the typically wide-ranging sources of Tippett's text and not to worry if everything does not make immediate sense. Since Tippett is once again his own librettist, literary and musical image go hand-in-hand. Allusions to and quotations from Jung, Shaw and Goethe may or may not illuminate Tippett's message just as suggestions of Beethoven, Ives and American popular music may or may not underline it.

The Ice Break is an obvious product of Tippett's acquaintance with America. From his first visit in 1965, the composer developed a strengthening affinity with American culture. The pace of life in the USA, the diverse cultural background of its peoples and, above all, the tensions in its society have stimulated his imagination. *The Knot Garden*, its offspring song-cycle, *Songs for Dov*, and, particularly, the Third Symphony (1970-72) are direct products of Tippett's American experience.

Tippett stresses anonymity in *The Ice Break* as it is an opera 'about stereotypes'. He does not name its setting but the resonances of the text tell us we are in an American city. The slang of the 'natives' is distinctively North American: music critics in the USA were noticeably touchy about its 'clumsiness' whereas English audiences may find it merely arch. The themes of the opera are those that obsess or at least permeate American culture: the polarity of Communist and capitalist political systems, the division between races attempting to co-exist in the same community, and the generation gap. The opera tackles these divisions head-on.

Further American themes and references are detectable. But Tippett's libretto suggests rather than stipulates — his concern is with the principles not the particulars — and what appears logically to be New York could, as Meirion Bowen has suggested,[1] as well be Belfast, Jerusalem or Johannesburg. The setting is ultimately irrelevant.

In Tippett's words the opera's subject is 'stereotypes — their imprisoning characteristics — and the need for individual rebirth'. These stereotypes are presented in stylised conflict with one another. There is hardly any scope for development of individual character: the pace of the opera and the hardening portrayal of stereotypes does not allow it. Only one character — Hannah, the black nurse — is allowed to break away from stereotyped behaviour, and it is she who is the catalyst for reconciliation and individual rebirth at the end of the opera.

The Characters in the Opera

Hannah is one of nine named characters and the only one who develops through the music she is given. Tippett conceived the six central characters as two groups with one person in common. The first group, of three, is a family. Lev, released after 20 years in prison and exile, arriving in a 'new world', suggests a Soviet dissident, perhaps a literary figure. Nadia, his wife (her name suggesting 'hope'), preceded him to a new home twenty years before. She is deeply nostalgic for her native land and has found reconciliation with her new surroundings difficult. Yuri, their son, is typical of some second generation immigrants: while disaffected with their parents' society, neither are they totally integrated with their new surroundings.

The second group is young: two black and two white. Olympion, 'a black champion', could be athlete or pop star but by his style of speech (and of song) is definitely in the Muhammed Ali mould. Hannah, his girl-friend, finds the sensationalism and, by implication, the violence and divisiveness of his character increasingly difficult to live with and searches for 'another way'. Gayle, Hannah's white girl-friend, on the other hand, identifies whole-heartedly with the black cause and in her naive liberalism, offers herself to Olympion. To Yuri, her boy-friend, this act is anathema and triggers off the explosive events that lead to his 'rebirth'. Being common to both groups Yuri is inevitably the symbol for reconciliation at the end.

There are three peripheral characters: a Police Lieutenant; Luke, the doctor; and Astron, the Messenger — but each is no more than a cipher. The chorus, however, has an importance in the drama on a par with the chorus in *The Midsummer Marriage*. In a note prefacing the text, Tippett writes:

> The chorus is always anonymous, whatever group it represents. It must be masked in some form, not only to enforce anonymity, but so that the stage presentation is unrelated to the singers' real body, in the sense

[1] Meirion Bowen, *Michael Tippett* (London, Robson Books, 1982), p. 81

that, for example, the traditional black-and-white minstrels might be played by Chinese. The masking is also necessary to show that stereotypes altogether are in question, rather than any presently exacerbated example e.g. 'black and white'.

Tippett's intention is to swamp the stage in the chorus scenes; indeed, he suggests that 'to obtain the imperatively necessary histrionic vitality in the chorus scenes, non-singing performers may have to be used'. In fact he even suggests that it might be possible to separate the 'imagined' source (the 'chorus' on stage) from the 'true oral source'.

Music and Sound
Electronic amplification plays an important role in the opera. Chorus scenes are literally 'amplified', made larger by offstage sounds. Amplification is used to suggest the distant voice of Lev in Nadia's mind, and, in an intelligent producer's hands, it could be employed effectively elsewhere. The composer certainly leaves scope for it. Electric guitars and electronic organ complement the otherwise traditional orchestra though Tippett stresses that the sound from their amplifiers must be merged into the orchestral ensemble in the pit. Despite their absorption into the orchestral texture there is no doubt that the electronically-amplified instruments increase the harshness of effect of prominent musical motifs in the opera.

Whether amplified or not, there are motifs (by which one could mean textures, or timbres, as well as particular combinations of notes and rhythms, or even combinations of all three) which have a particular force. In his note prefacing the score Tippett identifies 'two archetypal sounds: one related to the frightening but exhilarating sound of the ice breaking on the great northern rivers in the spring; the other related to the exciting or terrifying sound of the slogan-shouting crowds, which can lift you on their shoulders or stamp you to death'.

The Opera, Scene by Scene
Act One
Scene One: It is the sound of the breaking ice that opens the opera, suggesting the northern wastes that Lev is leaving and that Nadia remembers. Low grinding chords, followed by rhythmic manipulation of first a minor then a major third, suggest the frightening, jagged cracking of the ice floe:

[1]

It is a motif that is to return, readily recognisable, at crucial points in the score, while its musical constituents will be ever-present. Nadia and Yuri wait in the humming airport lounge for Lev's arrival. Nadia is half-ecstatic, half-fearful at the prospect. Yuri is surly, interrupting or answering his mother's comments with curt responses. To his embarrassment, Nadia (together with the audience) seems to hear Lev's voice over the ice-break motif. The parents' telepathic unity is shattered by the arrival of Gayle and Hannah.

Scene Two: The girls have come to greet Olympion. The music — fast and spiky — reflects Gayle's excitable, enthusiastic bluntness, while Hannah's sympathetic response to Yuri can be immediately detected in a floating cantabile line:

But she is swept up by Gayle's enthusiasm as they anticipate Olympion's arrival:

and their anticipation is underlined by the rising whole-tone motif in the orchestra:

Scene Three: Olympion's fans sweep into the airport lounge, engulfing everyone and everything, their whooping cries emphasised by a pounding rhythm. Hannah is swept off but Yuri confronts Gayle.

Scene Four: The confrontation is emphasised by harsh brass and percussion sounds. Gayle will not stand for Yuri's jealousy and leaves him, his mother and the airport lounge in relative peace.

Scene Five: Nadia's anxiety and Yuri's preoccupied mind are highlighted by the rather static accompaniment, giving the vocal lines the power of dramatic recitative. Underpinning the last seconds of the scene is a slow version of the rising whole-tone motif anticipating Olympion's arrival as the fans spill back onto the stage.

Scene Six: The chorus of Olympion's fans with their whoops and shouts herald their champion's arrival, even breaking into an American-style cheerleader routine, accompanied by suitably flamboyant, jazzy clarinet 'break' and side-drum rolls. Olympion acknowledges their greeting with his boastful declamations, set with a Monteverdian swagger that is coloured by the first solo use of electric guitar and electric bass guitar in the orchestra:

Hannah and Gayle are exhorted to unnecessarily exaggerated confirmation of his prowess, to music we have heard before (Ex. 3), again over fragments of the whole-tone motif. The fans sweep hero and hangers-on off the stage.

Scene Seven: Nadia now finds herself alone but gradually realises that the soberly-dressed stranger watching her is her husband. Lev greets her in the

Josephine Barstow as Gayle in the 1977 Covent Garden world première (photo: Zoë Dominic)

way she imagined in Scene One, musically, a rising cello phrase over low woodwind chords:

[6]

Nadia's response is again a mixture of ecstasy and nostalgia (the latter portrayed by low brass chords). The scene dissolves over the ice-break motif. Scene Eight: We find Nadia and Lev in her apartment. They tentatively explore each other's experiences, in accompanied recitative, heightened only by Nadia's uncontrolled relief and Lev's poetic musings:

[7]   LEV

Mention of Yuri disturbs their absorption in each other.
Scene Nine: The opera cuts back to the airport lounge where Olympion's fans continue their frenzied welcome. The scene proceeds as an exact repeat of words and music of Scene Six until Yuri is exhorted to join the paean of praise. His silence (marked by a pregnant orchestral pause) only generates inflammatory language from Olympion and a gradual separation of white fans from black. But Gayle, perversely, is now inspired (or provoked) into her own aria, not so much of praise but of cool, calculated, almost wanton sacrifice. It is an aria that makes fearsome technical demands on the singer: long-limbed

athletic lines combining flowing cantabile with the kind of spiky coloratura (echoed to thrilling effect by the trumpets) we already associate with Gayle:

[8]   GAYLE *(riding high over everyone present)*

Olympion is left in two minds while the chorus of fans is divided even further by Gayle's provocative act. As she throws herself at Olympion's feet, Yuri is unable to contain himself any longer, 'goes for' Olympion, and is felled, provoking the 'champion' to lash out at Gayle as well in rejection. The scene ends in tumult, with the amplified instruments adding to the deluge of sound. Scene Ten: Nadia and Lev have continued to discuss Yuri, it seems:

[9]

Lev reassures her that he will love and help his son. As he does so, the sound of the offstage chorus throws Yuri, dragging Gayle, into their room. Yuri's first contact with his father is a bitter, rhetorical question, half-spoken with nasal intonation, setting the seal on the confrontations that will erupt in Act Two.

Act Two

Scene One: Confrontation, and its devastating effect, is immediately evident. Lev, Nadia, Yuri and Gayle sing against each other, each with his or her own music, in an Ivesian collage, a technique employed by Tippett for the first (but not the last) time in the opera. First Lev tries reconciliation, to be rebuffed by Yuri; then Gayle rejects the dream of 'liberal charity' to which Yuri's parents have clung. The young ones are drawn away into the crowd of whites outside, to a sinister chromatic trumpet call. Nadia seems devastated by its implications whereas Lev retains a calm conditioned by twenty years of isolation and emotional discipline (Ex. 7).

Scene Two: The chorus of whites now fuses together singing music that is an uneasy combination of Methodist hymn, 'barber-shop' harmony and the sinister trumpet wailing from the end of the previous scene. This, their words and the white masked figures suggest Ku-Klux-Klan.

Scene Three: Olympion, accompanied and identified as always by the electric gùitars, tries to persuade Hannah that he must side with the blacks in their confrontation. Hannah cannot agree, but is herself wrestling with the dilemma and hints at the longer and deeper self-examination that is to come:

[10]   HANNAH

Scene Four: To a clearly jazz-orientated accompaniment, the black chorus sweep Olympion into their midst and, giving him no choice, mask him like themselves. The orchestra, with brilliant semiquaver flourishes in woodwind and strings and a ferocious outburst on tom-toms and piano, vividly depicts the mood of the mob the chorus has become.

Scene Five: We reach the heart of the opera. Hannah's aria is in the Tippett tradition of crucial, introspective solo scenes for female voices: Sosostris in *The Midsummer Marriage*, Helen in *King Priam* and Denise in *The Knot Garden* are the obvious precursors. Here, Hannah searches for some sense amid the violence. Her calm compassion is anticipated by a luminous orchestral passage, essentially a trio for oboes and harp, coloured at points by woodwind and string chords. Hannah's entry is marked by a distinctive octave leap and a change of orchestral colour as flutes supersede oboes and electric guitar the harp.

[11]   HANNAH

Stran — — — — — ger and

Something of Hannah's searching is conveyed by the way Tippett emphasises three adjacent notes (E, F and F sharp) as important tone centres. A brief agitated central section breaks away from these centres as Hannah doubts that any sense can yet be found. But her inner 'incommunicable voice' reasserts that there *is* hope, and the music, by returning to the three key tones and by resolving on a chord of C that contains the major and minor thirds of the ice-break motif, confirms this. We are left in no doubt that, as Andrew Porter put it,[2] it is in Hannah's 'kindly hands, generous soul, and distinctive compassion for all kinds of suffering [that] the composer discerns a limited chance for healing some of the world's divisions'.

Scene Six: Almost before Hannah has finished, the black and white mobs interrupt her calm. This is a scene of ritual confrontation. Tippett depicts 'the final, surrealist process of tribalisation' with another Ivesian collage. There are four elements. First, the ferocious tom-toms from the end of Scene Four mark the mobs' confrontation. Then each mob is characterised by 'tribal'

[2] Andrew Porter, 'A Composer of Our Time', *The New Yorker*, September 19, 1977, pp. 121-126.

music: the whites by 'Blue Mountain' fiddling, the blacks by voodoo-style shrieks on the clarinet:

[12]

Both of these are extended when combined, each clinging to its own key centre (whites in D, blacks on A flat) to emphasise their division. The choruses' shouts of hate for each other — the fourth element — are, however, disconcertingly similar. The elements are combined in a wild dance that catapults us again into a scene of relative calm.

Scene Seven: Nadia and Lev's temporary uncertainty is conveyed by their disjointed, unrelated ramblings and the hesitant patchwork of sound from the orchestral percussion. Nadia feels impotent, pessimistic; Lev resolutely

Luke (John Dobson) and Hannah (Beverly Vaughn) help Yuri (Tom McDonnell) to his feet, Covent Garden, 1977 (photo: Zoë Dominic)

questions his pacifist principles; yet their conclusion is simultaneous and unanimous, and Lev goes out into the night to seek for Yuri.

Scene Eight: Confrontation erupts to fiercely clashing seconds in the orchestra and heavy foot-drumming on the stage floor. Gunshots bring sudden silence before retaliatory shots leave one black and two white figures prostrate, and the wail of police sirens creeps into the musical void. It is possibly no accident that this scene vividly recalls — in sound and dramatic structure — the fatal confrontation of the New York gangs of Jets and Sharks in Bernstein's *West Side Story*.

Scene Nine: The Police Lieutenant is immediately and simultaneously provocative and resigned. He challenges the audience to take sides, his brashness emphasised by the orchestral brass. Luke, the doctor ('the divine physician'?) unmasks each body in turn. The first two are dead (Wozzeck's flat, passionless groan over Marie's body in Berg's opera is surely evoked here) and to Luke's horror and Hannah's distress, Olympion and Gayle are revealed. To the policeman they are merely bodies to be disposed of. Lev arrives on the scene as Yuri is discovered under the third mask. Yuri is crushed but alive. Luke seems to think he may live to experience pain and suffering again and suggests Lev should seek consolation from Hannah rather than go to the hospital with his son's broken body.

Scene Ten: Left alone, Hannah and Lev are drawn together in their mutual sorrow. Tippett portrays this without words, solo violin and cello clearly identifying the characters:

[13]

The gently rocking rhythm (apparently suggested by the final bars of the slow movement of Brahms's First Piano Concerto) conveys the comfort drawn from each other, and, in the way cello takes over from violin for a time, suggests that Lev has indeed drawn strength from Hannah's extraordinary willpower.

Act Three

Scene One: Lev reads to Nadia on her sickbed; the passage from Goethe's *Wilhelm Meister* anticipates the reconciliation of father and son, a significance not lost on Lev whose realisation is mirrored by gradually-rising bass *glissandi*.

Scene Two: Luke and Hannah are greeted by brave questions from Nadia about Yuri's health, whereas four bars on flutes and horns, drawn from Scene

124

Clyde Walker as Olympion and Beverly Vaughn as Hannah at Covent Garden in 1977 (photo: Zoë Dominic)

Ten of the previous act, tell us that Luke's enquiry after Nadia's health has an unwanted answer:

[14]

Luke and the gentle woodwind lines implore Nadia to relax. But, with clarinets and horns recalling the final scene of Act One (Ex. 9), Nadia asks Hannah to 'look for Lev' when she's gone. She sees him 'stand in my place' and her final fantastic vision begins.

Scene Three: Troubled by Nadia's state of mind, Lev is in uncharacteristic despair. Prompted by Hannah, he recalls his pacific acceptance of detention and exile and questions whether, as Yuri challenged, he 'flunked the struggle'. Hannah reflects that there are many struggles in the world, many ghettos, from which rebirth must be the prime aim. Musically, this scene presents a contrast between Lev's anguished melismatic cries with their contradictory defiant endings (whole-tone scalic phrases) and Hannah's positive response, with the brass underlining her rhetorical questions.

Scene Four: Nadia's fantastic vision interrupts them. Her childhood is vividly recalled in a brilliant orchestral evocation of running sleigh in snow-bound forest. She remembers the ice breaking on the river (and the sound, sure enough, is there in the orchestra) and (as she drifts into death) the idyllic summers.

Scene Five: As Lev cries out, a paradise, probably far from the one he imagines, is conjured up. Just as answers were being sought, Tippett chooses to question the easy solutions, represented in this scene by the fatuous questions of the 'Seekers', their drug-dependence and their naive acceptance of the psychedelic messenger and his ironic offer of hope (a quote from Jung).

Jazz kit and electronic instruments suggest the naivety and (with piano) the imagined storm in the Seekers' minds. Astron materialises to ethereal bell-like percussion sounds. To give it god-like qualities, his voice is represented by mezzo and counter-tenor together (shades of God's voice in Britten's *Abraham and Isaac*) and amplified for clarity of words:

When the Seekers, with great agitation mirrored in the orchestral brass parts, read too much into Astron's message, the messenger (in a rising, spoken falsetto) debunks his own role and disappears. The concept of this scene is risky, as the composer acknowledged before the première: the purpose — to point to the rejection of all ideologies that cause or have caused conflict in the world — is clear. But the method is too glib in the context of the final act.

Scene Six: Luke persuades Lev that his responsibility is not with Nadia any more, but with Yuri. Lev, despite the tugs on his conscience represented by familar horn and trumpet motifs (based on Ex. 14) responds positively.

Scene Seven: Nervous, anticipatory music from flutes and clarinets heralds the operation on Yuri, encased, egg-like, in plaster. The individual preoccupations of Lev (waiting outside the theatre), Yuri (anxious, apprehensive) and Luke and Hannah (matter-of-fact and professional) are again encapsulated in a musical collage, broken as Yuri bursts from the plaster. His physical rebirth — marked harmonically in the orchestra by the ice-break motif's chords in the brass — has many metaphorical resonances: freedom and the coming of spring are made obvious.

Scene Eight: As if to reinforce this, the Chorus from the Paradise Garden whirls through the hospital, repeating Astron's blessing stressing how the season of harvest is also the time of seed generation.

Scene Nine: The nervous motif on flutes and clarinets that opened Scene Seven now preludes Yuri's first steps. As he stands and proves himself whole again (reborn) the ice-break motif in its full orchestral glory (Ex. 1) marks not only his rebirth but his reconciliation with Lev. And another important motif on flutes, trumpets and violins, heard first in Act One, Scene Seven as Nadia and Lev were restored to each other, now tells us that Nadia's dream, that husband and son would be reconciled, is fulfilled. Hannah and Lev, however, caution against over-optimism. Over searing orchestral chords, that are at once concord and discord (Ex. 7) Lev quotes Goethe: for there to be resolution there must be conflict. The orchestra holds to its conflicting chords as the curtain falls. For us, Tippett is telling us, there can be no easy answers.

The Ice Break

An Opera in Three Acts by Michael Tippett
Libretto by Michael Tippett

Dedicated to Colin Davis

The Ice Break was first performed at The Royal Opera House, Covent Garden on July 7, 1977. The first performance in the United States was at the Savoy Theater, Boston on May 18, 1979.

CHARACTERS

Lev *50 year old teacher, released after 20 years' prison and exile*	bass
Nadia *his wife, who emigrated with their baby son*	lyric soprano
Yuri *their son, a student and second generation immigrant*	baritone
Gayle *Yuri's present and native-born white girl friend*	dramatic soprano
Hannah *Gayle's black friend, a hospital nurse*	rich mezzo
Olympion *Hannah's boy friend, a black champion*	tenor
Luke *a young intern at Hannah's hospital*	tenor
Lieutenant *a lieutenant of police*	baritone
Astron *a psychedelic messenger*	lyric mezzo & high tenor (or counter tenor)

Chorus of various groups

NOTE

Music
In the music there are two archetypal sounds; one related to the frightening but exhilarating sound of the ice breaking on the great northern rivers in the spring; the other related to the exciting or terrifying sound of the slogan-shouting crowds, which can lift you on their shoulders in triumph or stamp you to death.

The Language
When Lev and Nadia converse together in English and not in their mother-tongue, that is literary convention. With other characters the slang English used at times is closer to North American usage than, say, British or Australian.

Chorus
The chorus is always anonymous, whatever group it represents. It must be masked in some form, not only to enforce anonymity, but so that the stage representation is unrelated to the singers' real bodies, in the sense that, for example, the traditional black-and-white minstrels might be played by Chinese. The masking is also necessary to show that stereotypes in general are in question, rather than any presently exacerbated example e.g. 'black and white'. In a chorus scene the whole stage is occupied and any extant non-chorus scene totally submerged, even though when the chorus goes, the non-chorus scene appears once more still in progress. From this it follows that however much the dramatic action seems to move at times towards verisimilitude, this stage 'reality' is constantly splintered by a complimentary 'surrealism'. To obtain the imperatively necessary histrionic vitality in the chorus scenes, non-singing performers may have to be used. Indeed it might be possible, if it were appropriate, to separate the true oral source of vocal sound from the imagined, or histrionic source, altogether.

Amplification
There are two separate systems of amplification: for voices; for instruments. The microphones for voices will be placed on stage, backstage, or attached to the singers as required. The loud-speakers will sound generally as from the stage or, if necessary, from the auditorium.

Electronic instruments can be placed where the conductor wants. The sound from their amplifiers, however, *must* be merged into the orchestral ensemble in the pit. The amplification therefore (not the instruments) must be placed accordingly.

Note: the numbers in square brackets refer to the music examples in Leslie East's article.

'Frères humains, qui après nous vivez,
n'ayer les coeurs contre nous endurcis.'

'Brother humans, who will live after us,
do not harden your hearts against us.'

Act One

Scene One. *The hum of a vast airport lounge-hall.* [1]

NADIA

Years back,
When I first brought you to this land,
We came by ship.
Oh, those terrifying waves!
Now he comes to us by plane.
Your father flies to us like a homing-bird.
He won't fear those terrifying waves!

YURI

(*shouting above some incoherent announcement over the loudspeakers*)

He won't see them; he'll be too high.

NADIA

Aren't you excited, Yuri?
To see your father.
Twenty years of camp and exile.

YURI

No. I can't remember.

NADIA

I remember,
As it were yesterday.
I see him always.
I see him now,
Flying to us like a bird.

YURI
(*half-shouting*)

Keep your feet on this earth, momma!

NADIA

I see him. I hear him.
He's speaking to me now.
Lev, Lev, what is it?

YURI
(*over another burst of the loudspeakers*)

O Jesus Christ!

LEV

(*off stage through the loudspeakers where the scrambled announcement gives way to his voice*)

I came from exile in the spring,   [6]
As the ice was breaking on the rivers.
I've heard that sound so many years upon
    years of despair;

But now with hope.
O my Nadia:
Do you remember how we sauntered by the
    flowing river?

NADIA

I remember, I remember.

LEV

How we hugged and kissed in the spring
    sunshine?

NADIA

I remember, I remember.

The airport hum takes over from Lev's voice on the speakers and swamps Nadia's.

Scene Two.

GAYLE

Look, Hannah, there's young Yuri.
Hi, Yuri, why here? How come?

YURI
(*bitterly*)

My mother's over there:
In one of her trances.
We've come to meet my father.

GAYLE

I never knew you had a father.

HANNAH

Oh yes, he has.   [2]
Nadia has often told me.
Years of prison for some no-crime.

YURI

Do me a favour:
Keep your nose clean of my affairs.
And that was years ago when I was three.
        (*half-shouted*)
Cowards, they let themselves be stamped
    on.
            (*natural voice*)
We're different now.

GAYLE

You needn't shout our Hannah down,
She's on the world's top.
Hail to Olympion, the hero.   [3]
'Ain't that so', Hannah?

129

HANNAH

My man flies home in triumph. [4]

GAYLE

Look out! The fans!

Scene Three. *The fans, mostly black, some white, fill the stage, submerging everything, shouting and dancing, with rattles and toy-trumpets, the latter possibly pre-taped over the loudspeakers.*

FANS

Olá, Oló, Olympion!
          (*some voices shouted*)
Yeh! Yeh!
Hi-ya, Hannah, hi-ya.
Olá, Oló, Olympion!
Yeh! Yeh!
Come on, Gayle.
Let's go!

When they go they sweep Hannah away with them.

Scene Four.

YURI

Gayle, stop!
Why d'you fool around with Hannah and the blacks?

GAYLE

What's bugging you, man?
Cool and jivey once;
Now, touchy and tight.
You're a drag, Hannah's with it — and the others.

The loudspeakers announce an arrival. Gayle hurries after Hannah and the fans.

YURI
(*as though shouting after her*)

And Olympion, that black bastard.

Scene Five. *The airport hum takes over. Yuri stands sullen and pensive till Nadia jogs him.*

NADIA

Yuri, Yuri, I need you.

YURI
(*inattentive, as though with his ears cocked for sounds from fans off stage*)

What is it?

NADIA

Is the plane late?

YURI

Probably.
Have they announced it?

NADIA

Where were you? Who were you with?

YURI

Gayle and Hannah.

NADIA

Is the plane late?

YURI

Probably.
Have they announced it?

Offstage cheering.

NADIA

What's all that cheering?
Is it for Lev?

YURI

No, Olympion.

NADIA

Is the plane late?

YURI
(*half-shouting, directly at his mother, in exasperation*)

I don't know.

Scene Six. *The stage is once more submerged by the fans, returning with Olympion, Gayle and Hannah.*

FANS

Olá, Oló!
          (*shouted*)
Yeh! Yeh!

A cheer-leader and some of the fans prepare to put on one of those half-embarassing, half-comic, cheer-leader acts.

CHEER-LEADER AND FANS
(*throwing their bodies from side to side*)

Oli . . . Olá . . . Oló
Olù, Olympion.
Our ché, chá, chá, chú, chí,
Our champion.

OLYMPION
(*acknowledging the act with flamboyant good-humour*)

I'm beautiful: I'm black: [5]
I am unbeatable.

FANS

Champion!

OLYMPION

I'm beautiful: I'm black:
I am unbeatable.
'Ain't that so', Hannah? [3]

'Sure is so', Olympion.   [4]

OLYMPION

'Ain't that so', Gayle?

GAYLE

'Sure is so', Olympion.

FANS

Olá, Oló!
(shouted)
Yeh! Yeh!

As the stage clears of fans and their hero, the hum of the airport lounge takes over.

Scene Seven. *Nadia finds herself alone, for Yuri has gone. She looks round in great distress. A soberly dressed man, clearly a traveller, is watching her. When their eyes at last meet, there is a slow recognition.*

LEV

Nadia, Nadia,   [6]
I am your husband.

NADIA

Lev, my little Lev,
You flew to me like a bird.

They embrace. Behind the music the airport lounge dissolves into . . .

Scene Eight. *. . . Nadia's tiny apartment, where she and Lev can feel as intimate as they need.* [1]

NADIA

And the camps? The prison? The exile?
Ah, I should have stayed there with you:
Though I saw this country in a vision.

LEV

No, no — you saw right.
We alone survived the camps who had no
    ties, no family.
But you and . . .
            (scanning her face)
You were safe.
Was it hard?

NADIA

At first.
No dream, Lev,
A rough country.
But we . . .
(checking herself in apprehension, then hurrying on)
Not cruel like it was there for you.
Alive! A miracle!

LEV

Poetry upheld me.

(quoting)
'The earth was worth ten heavens to us.' [7]

NADIA

I dreamed of heaven.
But when he, when he grew up, the earth
    was kinder.

LEV

So Yuri is grown-up.
What kind of man?

NADIA
(crying out)
Do not ask me, Lev.
What does father or mother mean to him?

Scene Nine. *The stage is once more submerged by the fans, with Hannah, Olympion, Gayle and Yuri. There is food, probably, certainly drink. The cheer-leader does his act with his group.*

FANS
(shouted)

Yeh, Yeh, Yeh, Yeh.
(throwing their bodies from side to side)
Olí . . . Olá . . . Oló . . .
Olú . . . Olympion!
Our ché chá chá chú chí,
Our champion.

OLYMPION
(acknowledging the act with flamboyant good humour)

I'm beautiful: I'm black.   [5]
I am unbeatable.
'Ain't that so', Hannah?

HANNAH

'Sure is so', Olympion.

OLYMPION

'Ain't that so', Gayle?

GAYLE

'Sure is so', Olympion.

OLYMPION

'Ain't that so', Yuri?

FANS

Answer! Answer!
Yeh, Yeh, Yeh, Yeh!
Answer! Answer!
Yeh, Yeh, Yeh, Yeh, Yeh, Yeh!

OLYMPION

Screw him, he's a loser!
What can that cat do to me . . .

FANS

Nothing,
But nothing.

OLYMPION

... the greatest?

FANS

Mighty Olympion,
The black man's champion!

OLYMPION

My folks have lived this land
More years than any Paddy-Ivan.

FANS

A-ha!

OLYMPION

My folks have lived this land
Most years 'slong as Waspy-Whitey.*

FANS

O-ho!

OLYMPION

So now we want our birth-right.

FANS

Yeh, Yeh, Yeh, Yeh!

OLYMPION

Who will claim it?

FANS

Mighty Olympion, the black man's
champion.

OLYMPION

I am the greatest.

FANS

Yeh, Yeh, Yeh, Yeh!

OLYMPION

The Lord's a black man.

FANS

Yeh, Yeh, Yeh, Yeh, Yeh, Yeh!

OLYMPION

And Whitey gotta pay.

FANS

Pay!

OLYMPION

'Ain't that so', Hannah?

HANNAH

'Maybe is so', Olympion.

OLYMPION

'Ain't that so', Gayle?

GAYLE

'Sure is so', Olympion.

YURI
(*unable to contain himself in bitter mockery*)

'Sure is so', Olympion!

*Bit by bit the white fans have stopped the
slogan-singing and have drawn together in a
small group with Yuri.*

WHITES

Get her away, Yuri,
Get her away.

GAYLE
(*singing high over everyone present*)

Olympion,   [8]
Your people have lived this land as long as
    mine,
Olympion.
But not in freedom: not as equals:
Not with love.
That's past, Olympion:
I make amends.
We are the new New World.
'Make love not war.'
And as a pledge, Olympion,
Come kiss me now, black beauty,
Kiss.

OLYMPION
(*half-recoiling, half-desiring*)

Wow! This chick wants balling!

BLACKS

Ball her, Olympion, ball her.

HANNAH

Gayle's runnin' wild,
A devil's in her ...

BLACKS

Ball her, Olympion, ball her.
Massa ball his slave.
Ho! Ho! Ho! Ho!

HANNAH

... Take command, Olympion,
Take command;
Before the devil's in us too
And we all go under.

WHITES

Get her away,   Go for him!
Get her away,   Go for him!
Drag her away!   Go for the nigger!
Drag her away!   Go for the nigger!

GAYLE

I make amends,
Superstar Olympion,
I make amends.

---

* W.A.S.P.: White Anglo-Saxon Protestant

Gayle goes down on her knees before Olympion and her hair would seem to cover his feet.

YURI
(manic with rage)

You mother-fucking bastard.

Yuri goes for Olympion, who, without moving, lands him one on the jaw, so that Yuri falls flat. Olympion looks down for a moment at Gayle, then kicks her off with one clean movement.

OLYMPION

Trash!

BLACKS

Out, out!
Whitey out, Whitey out!
Out, out!
Whitey out, Whitey out!
Out, out, out, out, out, out, out, out.
Ou-t!

Scene Ten. *Nadia's apartment*

NADIA

He is so strange these days: [9]
Now dead, now wild.

LEV

Where is he now?

NADIA

I wouldn't know.
I used to.
But I love him, Lev,
I love him.
And you will love him.

LEV

For sure.

NADIA

And you will help him.

LEV

For sure, Nadia, for sure.

CHORUS
(off stage)

Out, out, out, out, out, out, out!
Ou-t!

Yuri bursts in dragging Gayle with him. He stares at his father, almost with hatred.

YURI
(half-spoken)

What have you come here for?

Curtain.

John Shirley-Quirk as Lev and Heather Harper as Nadia in the 1977 world première at Covent Garden (photo: Zoë Dominic)

133

Act Two

Scene One. *The city at night. As soon as the stage becomes visible, showing the apartment, Lev, Nadia, Yuri and Gayle at once start singing together, each in their private world.*

LEV
(*quoting*) [7]

'...Who am I to bear the burdens of this
   world:
To be the boss,
The navel of the earth,
Let alone the salt ...'

NADIA

Like him
I have hoped, I have endured
In the dungeons of this town.
Because I see the river
Shining with light as it cleaves the forest.

GAYLE

For me no bible-belted-safe plantation.
Footloose, I
(With my lover along)
Fool around
For kicks!

YURI

To hell with where one's born!
Haven't I grown to be a man here?
So, listen, while I shout in your stuffed ears:
Stop crowding me!

LEV
(*breaking out of the ensemble*)

Let me speak.
Violence is blind.
Brutality takes over.
I have experience.

YURI

You've no experience.
Twenty years locked up because you
   wouldn't fight.
Here it's different.
We're not pushed around.
Every guy has a gun.

MEN'S VOICES
(*off stage echoing through the speakers*)

Every guy has a gun,
Has a gun, has a gun.

LEV
(*quoting*)

'...Who am I to bear the burdens of this
   world:
To be the boss,

The navel of the earth,
Let alone the salt ...'

NADIA

Crazy and cruel now the earth is.
Like him
I have hoped, I have endured
In the dungeons of this town.
Because I see the river
Shining with light as it cleaves the forest.

GAYLE

For me no bible-belted-safe plantation.
Footloose, I
(With my lover along)
Fool around
For kicks!

YURI

To hell with where one's born!
Haven't I grown to be a man here?
So, listen, while I shout in your stuffed ears!
Stop crowding me!

GAYLE
(*breaking out of the ensemble*)

No dream now of liberal charity.
Now is for real.
'Burn, baby, burn!'

WOMEN'S VOICES
(*off stage echoing through the speakers*)

Burn, baby, burn, baby, burn, baby, burn!

GAYLE

What does that mean?
That I be killed?
We'll fight first.

LEV

The others can say all that: for ever.
So the toughest bully wins.
You, how brutal can *you* be?

YURI

Listen to the preaching teacher.
You can't teach us.

GAYLE AND YURI

We're through.
Now is for real.

NADIA

Crazy and cruel now the earth is.

The assembly call at first rivets their attentions; then Gayle and Yuri, as in a ritual, put on the hoods.

134

NADIA
(*crying out with visionary intensity*)

I see, I see
The Dance of Death
Whirling over the city.
Who dies? Who dies?

*Nadia goes. The two hooded figures begin
perhaps to recede, but always visible and
facing the audience. Lev seems to be left
behind, alone.*

LEV
(*quoting*)

'A frozen foot-cloth is the scarf that binds
my face.'

Scene Two. *As the masked figures of Gayle
and Yuri move backwards, a similarly
masked white chorus moves forward. They
all meet and leave the stage.*

CHORUS OF WHITES

We meet with cordial greetings
In this our sacred cave,
To pledge anew our compact,
With hearts sincere and brave.
A band of pure Caucasians,
The noblest of the Klan,
We stand in rank together,
White woman with white —

Scene Three. *Olympion and Hannah are
alone, as though in some other part of the
night city.*

OLYMPION

I must go with them.
If they 'walk tall', I walk taller.
I am their god, their hero.
I'm their man.

HANNAH

And I'm a woman.
But no, no:
Stranger and deeper why I stay.   [10]

HANNAH AND OLYMPION

What is so strange and deep as love,
Lover leaning to lover in the spring?

OLYMPION

Desert our brothers in trouble,
Run out on them?
Afraid to tangle with Whitey
Now the heat is on?

HANNAH

Whitey is human too.
But no, no:
Too glib, too pat.
Stranger and deeper into myself.   [10]

HANNAH AND OLYMPION

What is so strange and deep as love,
Lover leaning to lover in the spring?

OLYMPION

Come with me, my babe, my honey,
My Hannah, come with me.

CHORUS OF BLACKS
(*as though shouting and singing in the
distance and coming nearer*)

Out, out!
Out, out, out, out, out, out! Whitey out,
   Whitey out!

HANNAH

But is it you, Olympion,
Is it you, within this mob?

Scene Four. *As Hannah cries her last
question the black masked chorus appears to
surge onto the stage. They surround Olympion
and ceremoniously mask him into one of the
mob.*

CHORUS OF BLACKS

Hi, there, black man!
Olympion!
Hi, there, black man!
Olympion!
Hi, there, black man!
Our fist, our boot, our hammer.
Our fist, our boot, our hammer.
He'll flick that Whitey out;
He'll flick that Whitey out.

*The masked chorus prepares to surge or
march off, taking Olympion, now in-
distinguishable, with them. The effect is of a
crowd disappearing rapidly into the distance.*

CHORUS OF BLACKS

Out, out, Whitey out, Whitey out.
Out, out, Whitey out, Whitey out,
Out, out, out, out, out, out.
Burn, baby, burn!
Burn, baby . . .

Scene Five.

HANNAH

Stranger and darker,   [11]
Deeper into myself.
Blue night of my soul,
Blue-black within this city's night
I scrabble for unformed letters
That might make a word
To speak sense
To the blue night of my soul,
Blue-black within this city's night.
But no;
No time is yet for sense.
Alone,
Deep in the body:

Dark in the soul:
An incommunicable voice murmuring:
Not that, only not that.

CHORUS OF WHITES
(off stage)

... the noblest of the Klan ...

CHORUS OF BLACKS
(off stage)

... baby, burn! ...

Scene Six. *The hooded or masked mobs of Blacks and Whites appear on the stage from opposite sides to enact the final, surrealist process of tribalisation.* [12]

CHORUS OF BLACKS

... Burn, baby, burn!

CHORUS OF WHITES

... We stand in rank together,
white woman with white ...

The tribal dancing begins.

CHORUS OF WHITES

Wá-wá-wá-wá-wá-wá-white
wá-wá-wá-wá-wá-wá-woman
with wá-wá-wá-wá-wá-wá-white!

CHORUS OF BLACKS

B, b, b, b, b, burn
b, b, b, b, b, baby
b, b, b, b, b, b, b, b,
burn!

Scene Seven. *Lev and Nadia in the apartment. They have temporarily lost all certainty, whether of vision or philosophy. They mutter together in a kind of cat's-cradle of unspoken tensions.*

NADIA
(half-spoken, half-sung)

Who dies, who dies?
Alas, alas,
I cannot see.
For the inner eye is gotten shut
Tight, blind,
By the weird power that lifts them open.
And if I saw who dies
How could I hurl a warning
'Cross the blank gulf from age to youth?
Who would heed?
Lev, Lev, it falls to you.

LEV

'No dream of liberal charity', she said.
'Now is for real.'
Is her passion then more real than my
    patience?
Must I despise the liberal charity I live by?
I have no gun.
I cannot shoot.

But they, with fierce vitality,
They shoot each other.
Or if they could together
Shoot away this rotten world ... ?
I go with my bare hands.

Lev rushes out into the night.

Scene Eight. *The Black mob has someone from the White mob on the ground, writhing and crawling, and is kicking him to death. Each entry of the boot proceeds with a heavy thud and scream (amplified if need be by other voices) from the body on the ground. Some revolver shots from one side. The Blacks scatter except one, to the other side. This single figure stays beside the prostrate body on the stage to deliver the final blow. Another shot brings him to the ground. Some Whites begin to creep forward from their side. One shot from the Black side of the stage. The Whites scurry to shelter except one, more imprudent than the rest, who reaches the first prostrate body and perhaps even tries to lift or drag it. Prolonged volley of shots from the Black side of the stage; perhaps even from a sub-machine gun. The White figure falls.*
Police-car and ambulance sirens coming nearer and louder from the distance, till the headlamps are visible and we know that the cars have stopped and the personnel have got out.

Scene Nine. *The Lieutenant of Police strides down stage towards the audience.*

LIEUTENANT
(through loud-hailer)

Police — or fuzz?
Cops — or pigs?
You take your choice:
You on your ass out there.
    (matter-of-fact, natural voice)
Well, Doc Luke,
Who lives? Who lives?

LUKE
(beside the black body; spoken)

Dead.

The face is unmasked as Hannah comes closer.

Olympion!
    (to Hannah)
Oh you poor bastards,
'Gone with the wind.'
    (shouting)
For what?

HANNAH

What has more power of pain than love?

LIEUTENANT

To the mortuary!
(through loud-hailer to the world at large)

Trash!

Olympion's body is removed.

LUKE
(beside the second white body that fell; spoken)

Dead.

The face is unmasked.

Gayle!
The kid who died for kicks.
Gayle, bonny Gayle, gone out with the wind.

LIEUTENANT

To the mortuary!
(through the loud-hailer to the world at large)
Trash!

Gayle's body is removed. Luke is beside the third body which is finally unmasked.

LEV
(rushing forward)

Yuri!

LIEUTENANT

Back.
Who are you?

LEV

He is my son.

LIEUTENANT
(through the loud-hailer to the world at large)

What a father!

(natural voice to Lev)
Why in a'mighty hell not have kept him out of this?

LEV

Please, please, is he alive?

LUKE
(spat out)

If we make the hospital in time, he may live . . .
(bitterly)
. . . like us all.

LIEUTENANT

Ambulance.

LEV

I will come with you.

Yuri is lifted into the ambulance.

LUKE

No: tomorrow.
Turn to Nurse Hannah.

The cars with their burdens go off with sirens wailing into the distance.

Scene Ten. *The stage is empty except for the figures of Lev and Hannah seeking comfort for their sorrow. [13] Perhaps Lev, as the cello takes over from the violin for a time, decides to accept Luke's advice to turn to Hannah. [14]*

Curtain.

Act Two at Covent Garden, 1979 with (foreground) Elizabeth Vaughan as Gayle and Tom McDonnell as Yuri (photo: Zoë Dominic)

137

Act Three

Scene One. *Nadia is dozing in the apartment. Lev sits beside her reading.*

LEV'S VOICE
(*murmured over the loud-speakers*)

'Now the boat glided in the hot, noonday
sunshine, down-stream; gentle breezes . . .'

NADIA

Lev, Lev, when will they come?

LEV

Soon, Nadia, soon.
Lie still.

LEV'S VOICE
(*murmured*)

'. . . right above, on the sharpest edge of
such a cliff, where otherwise the towpath
might have passed . . .'

NADIA
(*murmuring*)

I cannot lie still.

LEV'S VOICE
(*murmured*)

'. . . saw a young man ride up, well built, of
powerful form . . .'

NADIA

Ah, but I need to know if Yuri lives.

*Lev perhaps lays a hand on Nadia's arm to
comfort her — but continues to read.*

LEV'S VOICE
(*murmured*)

'. . . but scarcely did they try to see him
more clearly, when the overhanging mass
there broke loose, and that unlucky youth,
horse over rider, plunged down into the
water.'

Scene Two. *Luke and Hannah have arrived.*

NADIA

How is he, doctor?

LUKE

Yuri is fine, just fine.
But what of you?

NADIA

Will Yuri walk again [14]
Upright like a man?

LUKE

We think so.
The test will come later.

NADIA

I shall not see that.

HANNAH

Indeed you will.
Rest now: relax.

Luke takes Lev aside.

NADIA

My dear soul,
You'll look for Lev, [9]
When I am gone.

HANNAH

I'll try — but . . .

NADIA

Since that crazed night,
And Yuri hovering between death and life,
I fall away into extinction.
(*stage trumpets in the distance*)
But now, but now I see, I see
Lev the Lion stand in my place.

*Nadia's face retains the look of visionary
ecstasy until the trumpets cease.*

Scene Three. *Hannah and Lev are together.
Luke perhaps is seen leaving.*

LEV
(*passionately*)

Why did I leave that other country?
(*imitating Yuri's sneering tone at the end of
Act One*)
What have I come here for?
(*bitterly*)
To watch my wife's death and my son's
hatred?

HANNAH
(*very distinct*)

That other country has troubles too. Tell
me.

LEV

Comrades
  In the camp
Against the brutal guards
  (Few felt them human too)
Totally single for survival.

I licked my wounds,
  In exile
Cringed into country quiet,
  Yet longed for the city.

The town seemed dead,
  Upon release,
The life conformist, empty.

(*crying out*)
Was Yuri right?
We flunked the struggle?
I ran away.
I ran away.
Ah! Ah!

HANNAH

Struggle is always,
Is here,
Here in this vast world of ghettos.
How to be reborn out of the ghetto?
On what deep level?

Scene Four. *Lev and Hannah are interrupted by the, for them, 'metaphorical'
sound of sleighbells as Nadia begins her
swan-song of death. The aria is fantasy, not
realism. Lev and Hannah are present, but
out of focus except when they comment.*

NADIA

Who holds me tight round the waist,
as the sleigh flies over the snow?
My brother? His school-mate?
Crowds of young comrades ski-ing,
skimming round the forest trees
with scarves flying.
I have felt-boots and a padded-coat.
But he holds me tight, warm,
as the sleigh stops sharp at the door.
The hot stoves glow red in the house.

LEV

How is she, Hannah?

HANNAH

Failing: very gently.

NADIA

They sleep; I wake.
Dark in the little room before dawn.
The night-light for us younger children has
     gone out.
I shan't need a night-light soon for my body
     changes.
Ahi, ahi,
Whatever's that?   [1]
The ice is breaking on the river.
Máma, Nánya, Lev,
Oh come, do come.

LEV

Is she in pain, Hannah?

HANNAH

No: the body shudders.
Death is near.

NADIA

I am walking through fields of marguerites
     in the hot, hot summer sun.
They reach my shoulders; my head peers
     out above.
Ah, I see far off the forest and the river.

What a tiny boat!
I glide downstream.
The wide water is full of folk,
Calling, calling . . .

CHORUS
(*off stage through loudspeakers*)

We are all here.
We are all here.

LEV
(*crying out*)

Nadia, Nadia, wait for me in Paradise.

Scene Five. *Seekers of all kinds, tough and
tender, past, present and future, are in the
Paradise Garden; perhaps smoking pipes of
peace or pot.*

CHORUS

Ready?
Am I ready?
Are you ready?
Are we all . . .
. . . ready . . .
for the trip?

If appropriate they puff out clouds of smoke.

What is that drumming, thrumming in the
     sky?
What is that rumbling, crumbling in the
     Earth?
A dadda-momma of a storm within the
     universe.

We could use
Some good News
From Nowhere right now.

Trekking from the farthest star,
Atoms, with the speed of light,
Assemble incarnate
Here.

*As the psychedelic colours reach their greatest
intensity, Astron materialises. The double
voice should be 'orchestrated', 'coloured', i.e.
given degrees of strangeness — even slight
distortion — according to the changes of
emphasis and meaning, by means of speaking-
tube and loud-speaker system or other
device, providing the words remain quite
clear.*

ASTRON

My letter to you is in code, not clear.
A tongue-slip that?
No matter.
'Dear friends,
Take care for the Earth.   [15]
God will take care for himself.'

CHORUS

Take care,
Ah, take care
For the Earth,
Our mother.

ASTRON

A blessing I remember
From an earlier dream:
'Spring come to you at the farthest
In the very end of harvest.'

CHORUS

Astron!
O Messenger!
Angel!
Our Saviour Hero!

ASTRON
(*highly ironic: rising into falsetto*)

Saviour?! Hero?! Me!!
(*natural voice*)
You must be joking.

*Astron's psychedelic image starts to tremble
and disintegrate to nothing.*

*Invisible, in the distance, as though from
the black hole where he appeared; through
the speakers:*

'Take care for the Earth.   [15]
God will take care for himself.'

*The Paradise Garden with the Chorus
vanishes as by ... explosion.*

Scene Six. *The quiet of Luke's consulting
room. From time to time Lev seems to hear
faint musical echoes, inaudible to Luke, from
Nadia's death scene.*

LUKE
(*distinct, serious but cool*)

Daily I deal with death ... and life.
The seriously sick move towards death,   [14]
Are accepted, are refused.
Or so it seems.
My skilled hands sometimes decide.
Or so it seems.
In the camps,
You too lived daily life with death,
Moved at times, I reckon, very close;
But were rejected.
You cannot be where Nadia is.
You are where Yuri is.
Your face changes.
Something has happened?

LEV

Yes.

LUKE

Are you then ready?

LEV

I am ready.

Scene Seven. *Some hall within the hive of
activity of a large hospital. (Lev and Luke
are possibly still visible where they were in
Scene Six.) Hannah wheels in Yuri, prone on*

*a mobile table. He is totally (at least meta-
phorically) encased in plaster.*

YURI

What happens now, Hannah?

HANNAH

At the crunch, Yuri,
Shouldn't you call me nurse?

YURI

Nurse Hannah, then.
What happens now?

HANNAH

We cut the plaster open,
And see the ghastly white flesh inside.

LUKE
(*approaching in his white coat*)

Is all set, Nurse?
And the patient ready?

YURI

Will you make me walk?

LUKE

Not yet; in time.

*Hannah wheels Yuri away into the operating
room. Luke follows.*

*The quartet-ensemble is surrealism, not
realism. Luke, Hannah, Yuri are within
(their voices may have to be amplified),
operating or suffering, as in some huge
shadow-play, an alarming but healing ritual.
Lev, now in the hall, is left alone in full view.*

LEV

Now his awareness concentrates,
Like waiting for interrogation.
His heart-beats quicken,
As the seconds lengthen in the mind to
     minutes,
And the minutes into hours.
O Yuri, does one ever walk
Again upright after interrogation?

HANNAH

No anaesthetic:
You'll feel no pain.

LUKE

Relax if possible.
The heart races.

YURI

Had I no nerves,
No apprehension,
All might be simple.
In this extremity
I fall like Momma into trance.

LUKE

Cutter: saw.

HANNAH

I have them ready.

LUKE

Then we begin.

LEV

Now they begin the beautiful operation.
With saw and cutter to crack the shell
To release the naked human chick
And test the skill
That soldered my Yuri's crushed bones
   together.
Surely a paean of triumph.
Oh moment of joy!

YURI

Ah-i! Ah-i!
Doctor, Nurse,
Take care for the fragile body
So white appearing.
Ah-i! Ah-i!
Dead-white and naked.
My body is free.
Joy, joy, joy!
Oy, oy, oy, oy!

LUKE

That plaster there;
Wrench it free.
Nurse, the cutters!
A birth like Caesar's, surely!
   (*with Hannah in triumph*)
The patient is free.
The patient is free.

HANNAH

There, I have it.
Ripe for the trash can.
   (*with Luke in triumph*)
The patient is free.
The patient is free.

Scene Eight. *With voices of Scene Seven still echoing around, the Chorus from the Paradise Garden whirls through the hospital like a carnival rout. Somersaults and cartwheels would be in order. Large untuned handbells to be clanged in time with the rhythmical words that are projected, as the Chorus enters, maybe through loud-hailers; within a general hum of voices which then take up the singing.*

CHORUS

'Spring, spring,
Spring come to you at the farthest,
In the very end of harvest.'

Scene Nine. *As the Chorus whirls away, Hannah brings a now robed Yuri out of the operating room in a wheel chair. She wheels him almost up to the standing Lev. Yuri stares at his father, intently searching his face.*

YURI
   (*with a touch of authority*)

Help me up, Nurse, Doctor.

     Luke and Hannah do so.

Let me go!
Let me stand!

Yuri stands, then takes some tentative steps.
[1]
Father!

LEV

Son!

     They embrace.

YURI

Chastened, together,
We try once more.
   (*drawing himself fully upright*)
'Ain't that so', Hannah?

He topples. Luke and Hannah help him back into the chair.

LUKE

You're sure not in balance yet.

   Hannah begins to wheel him away.

YURI
   (*unrepentant*)

But . . . 'ain't that so?'

HANNAH

Stop it!
Much deeper.
Oh, much deeper.

   Luke, Hannah and Yuri move on again.

LEV
   (*quoting*)

'Yet you will always be brought forth
   again,   [7]
(*as though in the far distance 'the horns of elfland faintly blowing'*)
   glorious image of God,
and likewise be maimed, wounded afresh,
   from within or without.'

     He turns to go after the others.

     Curtain.

Discography *by Cathy Peterson*

The Midsummer Marriage

Conductor	*C. Davis*
Orchestra/Opera House	**Royal Opera House**
Date	*1970*
Mark	A. Remedios
Jenifer	J. Carlyle
King Fisher	R. Herincx
Bella	E. Harwood
Jack	S. Burrows
Sosostris	H. Watts
He-Ancient	S. Dean
She-Ancient	E. Bainbridge
UK disc number	6703 027

King Priam

Conductor	*D. Atherton*
Orchestra/Opera House	**London Sinfonietta**
Date	*1980*
Priam	N. Bailey
Achilles	R. Tear
Hector	T. Allen
Paris	P. Langridge
Hermes	K. Bowen
Andromache	F. Palmer
Helen	Y. Minton
Hecuba	H. Harper
Nurse	A. Murray
UK disc number	D246D3
UK tape number	K246K33
US disc number	LDR 73006

The Knot Garden

Conductor	C. Davis
Orchestra/Opera House	**Royal Opera House**
Date	1973
Faber	R. Herincx
Thea	Y. Minton
Flora	J. Gomez
Denise	J. Barstow
Mel	T. Carey
Dov	R. Tear
Mangus	T. Hemsley
UK disc number	412-707-1
US disc number	412-707-1

At the time of writing, *The Ice Break* remains unrecorded. All three of the above recordings are highly recommended. For a detailed analysis of these recordings, readers are referred to John Steane's excellent article on 'English Opera in the Twentieth Century' in *Opera on Record 3* (ed. Alan Blyth, Hutchinson, 1984).

Bibliography

There are now several books about Tippett: Ian Kemp is the author of the major study, *Tippett: the Composer and his Music* (London, 1984), which contains both a biographical introduction and extensive and detailed discussions of all his work. There are shorter introductions by Eric Walter White (*Tippett and his Operas*, London, 1979), Michael Hurd (*Michael Tippett: a short biography*, London, 1978), David Matthews (*Michael Tippett, an Introductory Study*, London, 1980) and Meirion Bowen (*Michael Tippett*, London, 1981). *The Music of Britten and Tippett* by Arnold Whittall (Cambridge, 1982) is a masterly comparative study in musical analysis and *Michael Tippett: A Celebration* (The Baton Press, Tunbridge Wells, 1985) is a collection of original critical essays on the music.

It will be clear that relevant suggestions for background reading for Tippett's librettos would range from Aeschylus to contemporary pacifist literature. His own writings are collected in two volumes: *Moving into Aquarius* (London, 1958, 1974) and *Music of the Angels*, ed. Meirion Bowen (London, 1980).

Contributors

Meirion Bowen writes regularly on music for *The Guardian*, is active as a lecturer and piano accompanist, and is Tippett's main assistant and adviser. He is currently writing a study of Luciano Berio and a book on 20th-century music.

Paul Driver has written on music for numerous newspapers and journals. He spent 1983-84 as music critic for *The Boston Globe*.

John Lloyd Davies is a Staff Producer at English National Opera.

Andrew Clements is music critic of *The New Statesman* and also writes for *The Financial Times* and *Opera* magazine.

Leslie East is Director of Music at the Guildhall School of Music and Drama. He has written extensively on contemporary British music, in particular for the magazine *Music and Musicians*. Other writings include a chapter on Thea Musgrave and Gordon Cross in *British Music Now* and contributions to *The New Grove*.